Criminality
and Psychiatric Disorders

CRIMINALITY
AND
PSYCHIATRIC DISORDERS

Samuel B. Guze, M.D.

Spencer T. Olin Professor of Psychiatry
Head of the Department of Psychiatry
Vice-Chancellor for Medical Affairs
Washington University
School of Medicine
St. Louis, Missouri

New York
Oxford University Press
London   Toronto   1976

Dedicated to Joy

Acknowledgements

The work to be described in this volume covered fifteen years. It included more than a thousand research interviews, the review of thousands of files and records, and extensive data analysis. It could not have been done without the help of many individuals. First of all, Mr. Vearl Harris of the Missouri Board of Probation and Parole, whose enthusiasm, support, and full cooperation made everything else possible. Without his help and the help of his staff, nothing could have been done.

Through the years I have been very fortunate to have had the indispensable assistance of a number of young colleagues who, as psychiatric residents, tested their interest and capacity for psychiatric research by sharing in this enterprise. Noteworthy are Doctors Vincente Tuason, Mark Stewart, David Gatfield, Bruce Picken, Edwin Wolfgram, Robert Hicks, Dennis Cantwell, Donald Goodwin, Bruce Crane, and Robert Cloninger. Most have gone on to successful independent careers in academic medicine and research. The others are active practitioners.

Locating and persuading subjects to participate in the study, assembling and analyzing files and records, coding of interviews and records, preparing material for computer storage and analysis, and generally being helpful and thoughtful were the important assignments admirably carried out by research assistants Susan Stone, Rosalie Miller, Eunice Henry, Carol Dowd Gaskin, and Peggy Freedman.

Over the years, financial support for the various phases of the study came from different sources. The following grants were most important: AA-00209, MH-05804, and MH-19972.

And finally, the cheerful, conscientious, intelligent, dependable help of my secretary, Rita Bayer, deserves special recognition. Treating everyone with courtesy and good will and helping in every way possible, she has been a crucial member of the team.

S.B.G.

St. Louis
March 1975

Contents

Criminality

and Psychiatric Disorders

ONE
Introduction

The Nature and Scope of the Problem

Crime is one of the foremost problems in contemporary American society. Widespread concern about it inevitably shapes political, economic, and social decisions. Only certain costs of crime are definitely measurable: the value of stolen property and the expense of maintaining police forces, courts, prisons, parole offices, and private security forces. These amount to many billions of dollars each year. Other costs cannot be easily measured: loss of life, serious injury, deterioration of neighborhoods, public fear, and reduced freedom of movement.

General concern about crime stems from the striking increase in reported crime during the past fifteen years. Not all of the *reported* increase, however, is necessarily the result of an *actual* increase. Depending on the specific crime, several surveys indicate that actual crime may be anywhere from twice to ten times as frequent as reported crime. This means there is much room for an increase in the proportion of reported crimes to produce an apparent increase in crime rates.

As noted and discussed in a report of the President's Commission on Law Enforcement and Administration of Justice published in 1967 (80), changing attitudes and expectations in the community, changing police practices, and increased insurance coverage lead to increased reporting of crime:

> One change of importance in the amount of crime that is reported in our society is the change in the expectations of the poor and members of minority groups about civil rights and social protection. Not long ago there was a tendency to dismiss reports of all but the most serious offenses in slum areas and segregated minority group districts. The poor and the segregated minority groups were left to take care of their own problems. Commission studies indicate that whatever the past pattern was, these areas now have a strong feeling of need for adequate police protection. Crimes that were once unknown to the police, or ignored when complaints were received, are now much more likely to be reported and recorded as part of the regular statistical procedure.

> .   .   .

> Perhaps the most important change for reporting purposes that has taken place in the last 25 years is the change in the police. Notable progress has been made during this period in the professionalization of police forces. With this change, Commission studies indicate, there is a strong trend toward more formal actions, more formal records and less informal disposition of individual cases. This trend is particularly apparent in the way the police handle juveniles, where the greatest increases are reported, but seems to apply to other cases as well. It seems likely that professionalization also results in greater police efficiency in looking for crime. Increases in the number of clerks and statistical personnel, better methods for recording information, and the use of more intensive patrolling practices also tend to increase the amount of recorded crime. Because this process of professionalization has taken place over a period of time and because it is most often a gradual rather than an abrupt change, it is difficult to estimate what its cumulative effect has been.

> .   .   .

> Perhaps the clearest illustration of the impact that changes in reporting systems can have is that shown by the history of such changes in New York City and Chicago. These cities are two of the Nation's largest police jurisdictions, accounting in 1965 for 20 percent of all reported robberies and 7 percent of all reported burgla-

ries. Changes in their reporting systems have several times produced large paper increases in crime. . . .

Although Chicago, with about 3 million people, has remained a little less than half the size of New York City with 7½ million throughout the period covered . . . , it was reporting in 1935 about 8 times as many robberies. It continued to report several times as many robberies as New York City until 1949, when the FBI discontinued publication of New York reports because it no longer believed them. In 1950 New York discontinued its prior practice of allowing precincts to handle complaints directly and installed a central reporting system, through which citizens had to route all calls.

In the first year, robberies rose 400 percent and burglaries 1,300 percent, passing Chicago in volume for both offenses. In 1959 Chicago installed a central complaint bureau of its own, reporting thereafter several times more robberies than New York. In 1966 New York, which appeared to have had a sharp decline in robberies in the late fifties, again tightened its central controls and found a much higher number of offenses. Based on preliminary reports for 1966, it is now reporting about 25 percent more robberies than Chicago.

. . .

Another factor that probably increases the amount of reporting for some crimes is the sizable increase in insurance coverage against theft. It is difficult to evaluate this factor. However, because many persons believe that they must report a criminal event to the police in order to collect insurance, more reporting seems likely. Although not the only factor involved, one indication that this may be the case is the high rate of reporting for auto theft noted by the . . . survey. Insurance is usually involved in auto theft.

The Commission concluded, at the same time, that a number of factors related to crime have been changing in ways that would lead to real increases in certain crimes: changing age composition of the population, urbanization, increased affluence, and inflation.

One of the most significant factors affecting crime rates is the age composition of the population. In 1965 more than 44 percent of all persons arrested for forcible rape, more than 39 percent for robbery, and more than 26 percent for willful homicide and aggravated assault were in the 18- to 24-year-old age group. For property crimes the highest percentages are found in the under 18 group—nearly 50 percent of all those arrested for burglary and larceny and more than 60 percent for auto theft.

For most of these offenses the rate of offense per individual in these age groups is many times that in older groups. Of course the differences are based on arrest figures, and the national figures on offenses cleared by arrest show that 75 to 80 percent of burglaries, larcenies, and auto thefts are unsolved. It is possible that older persons committing offenses against property are more successful at evading arrest, so that the age figures for arrests give a somewhat biased picture.

Because of the unusual birth rate in the postwar years, the youthful high-risk group—those in their teens and early twenties—has been increasing much faster than other groups in the population.

. . .

Commission studies . . . indicate that between 1960 and 1965 about 40 to 50 percent of the total increase in the arrests reported by Uniform Crime Reports could have been expected as the result of increases in population and changes in the age composition of the population.

. . .

Rates for most crimes are highest in the big cities. Twenty-six core cities of more than 500,000 people, with less than 18 percent of the total population, account for more than half of all reported Index crimes against the person and more than 30 percent of all reported Index property crimes. One of every three robberies and nearly one of every five rapes occurs in cities of more than 1 million. The average rate for every Index crime except burglary . . . is at least twice as great—and often more—in these cities as in the suburbs or rural areas. With a few exceptions, average rates increase progressively as the size of the city becomes larger.

. . .

The country has for many years seen a steady increase in its urban population and a decline in the proportion of the population living in rural areas and smaller towns. Since 1930 the rural population has increased by less than 2 percent while the city population has increased by more than 50 percent. The increase in the cities and their suburbs since 1960 alone has been about 10 percent. Because of the higher crime rates in and around the larger cities, this trend toward urbanization has a considerable effect on the national rate for most Index crimes. Commission studies show that if metropolitan, small city, and rural crime rates for 1960 had remained constant through 1965, the increase that could have been expected due to urbanization would have been about 7 to 8 percent of the increase reported by the Uniform Crime Reports.

It would obviously tell us a great deal about the trend of crime if we could analyze all together the changes that have been taking place in urbanization, age composition of the population, number of slum dwellers, and other factors such as sex, race, and level of income. The Commission has spent a considerable amount of time trying to make this kind of analysis. However, it was unable to analyze satisfactorily more than one or two factors in conjunction with each other on the basis of present information.

. . .

On the basis of its study, the Commission estimates that the total expected increase in crime from 1960 to 1965 from these kinds of changes would be at least half, and possibly a great deal more, of the total increase in crime rates actually observed. The Commission's study clearly indicates the need for fuller reporting of arrest information and for the development of more compatibility between police statistics and information collected by other statistical agencies. The FBI has already made substantial progress in this direction in recent years but further steps are still needed.

. . .

Another change that may result in more crime is increasing affluence. There are more goods around to be stolen. National wealth and all categories of merchandise have increased in terms of constant dollars more than fourfold since 1940—significantly more than the population or the rate of reported theft.

Increased affluence may also have meant that property is now protected less well than formerly. More than 40 percent of all auto thefts involve cars with the keys inside or the switch left open. A substantial percentage of residential burglaries occur in unlocked houses. Bicycles, whose theft constitutes 15 percent of all reported larcenies, are frequently left lying around. Larceny of goods and accessories from cars accounts for another 40 percent of all reported larceny.

Some increased business theft seems directly due to less protection. The recent rise in bank robbery seems due in large part to the development of small, poorly protected branch banks in the suburbs.

7

In retail establishments, managers choose to tolerate a high percentage of shoplifting rather than pay for additional clerks. Discount stores, for example, experience an inventory loss rate almost double that of the conventional department store. Studies indicate that there is in general more public tolerance for theft of property and goods from large organizations than from small ones, from big corporations or utilities than from small neighborhood establishments. Restraints on conduct that were effective in a more personal rural society do not seem as effective in an impersonal society of large organizations.

Inflation has also had an impact on some property crimes. Larceny, for example, is any stealing that does not involve force or fraud. The test of the seriousness of larceny is the value of the property stolen. The dividing line between "grand" and "petty" larceny for national reporting purposes is $50. Larceny of $50 and over is the Index offense that has increased the most over the history of the Uniform Crime Reports, more than 550 percent since 1933. Because the purchasing power of the dollar today is only 40 percent of what it was in 1933, many thefts that would have been under $50 then are over $50 now. Uniform Crime Reports figures on the value of property stolen, for example, indicate that the average value of a larceny has risen from $26 in 1940 to $84 in 1965.

. . .

Because of the grave public concern about the crime problem in America today, the Commission has made a special effort to understand the amount and trend of crime and has reached the following conclusions:

1. The number of offenses—crimes of violence, crimes against property and most others as well—has been increasing. Naturally, population growth is one of the significant contributing factors in the total amount of crime.

2. Most forms of crime—especially crimes against property—are increasing faster than population growth. This means that the risk of victimization to the individual citizen for these crimes is increasing, although it is not possible to ascertain precisely the extent of the increase. All the economic and social factors discussed above support, and indeed lead to, this conclusion.

The Commission found it very difficult to make accurate measurements of crime trends by relying solely on official figures, since it is likely that each year police agencies are to some degree dipping deeper into the vast reservoir of unreported crime. People are probably reporting more to the police as a reflection of higher expectations and greater confidence, and the police in turn are reflecting this in their statistics. In this sense more efficient policing may be leading to higher rates of reported crime. The diligence of the FBI in promoting more complete and accurate reporting through the development of professional police reporting procedures has clearly had an important effect on the completeness of reporting, but while this task of upgrading local reporting is under way, the FBI is faced with the problem, in computing national trends, of omitting for a time the places undergoing changes in reporting methods and estimating the amount of crime that occurred in those places in prior years.

3. Although the Commission concluded that there has been an increase in the volume and rate of crime in America, it has been unable to decide whether individual Americans today are more criminal than their counterparts 5, 10, or 25 years ago. To answer this question it would be necessary to make comparisons between persons of the same age, sex, race, place of residence, economic status and other factors at the different times: in other words, to decide whether the 15-year-old slum dweller or the 50-year-old businessman is inherently more criminal now than the 15-year-old slum dweller or the 50-year-old-businessman in the past. Because of the many rapid and turbulent changes over these years in society as a whole and in the myriad conditions of life which affect crime, it was not possible for the Commission to make such a comparison. Nor do the data exist to make even simple comparisons of the incidence of crime among persons of the same age, sex, race and place of residence at these different years.

These excerpts from the Commission's report remain valid today. It is still not possible to estimate correctly the proportion of reported increases in crime represented by greater ascertainment rather than by actual increases in criminal behavior. The definite increase, however, in that segment of the population—young males—most likely to commit crimes means that more crimes are probably being committed and, therefore, that the risk of being a victim of crime has probably increased. Despite uncertainties and limitations in available data, this last observation indicates that the public's concern is at least partially justified.

Uncertainty about the significance of changing rates of reported crime from one year to the next is paralleled by similar difficulty in interpreting differences between various parts of the country.

To illustrate geographic variation in reported crime, it may be helpful to consider rates for murder and forcible rape from a number of the largest standard metropolitan statistical areas (SMSA's) as reported by the FBI (61). These two crimes are noteworthy in this context because murder is probably reported to the police in the great majority of cases, whereas rape is perhaps the most serious crime with the lowest proportion of cases reported to the police.

Rates for murder and rape in different metropolitan areas may vary ten- to fifteenfold. Some SMSA's report higher than average rates for both crimes, others lower than average rates for both crimes, but many report below average rates for one and above average for the other.

The national average in 1972 for all SMSA's was 9.9 per 100,000 population for murder and 26.9 per 100,000 for rape. Jacksonville, Florida, was among the highest for both crimes with rates of 17.4 for murder and 54.5 for rape. Milwaukee was low for both with rates of 4.3 for murder and 9.0 for rape. San Francisco, on the other hand, was only 8.6 for murder but 45.2 for rape, while Miami was 14.3 for murder and 21.2 for rape. These differences are not easy to explain.

Similarly, there is no obvious explanation for the fact that Albuquerque, Ann Arbor, Colorado Springs, Denver, and Santa Cruz were among those areas reporting the highest rates for rape, while Boston, Pittsburgh, Miami, and Milwaukee were among those with the lowest. And why did Indianapolis, Denver, Cincinnati, Kansas City, San Francisco, and Pittsburgh report murder rates below the national average, while Cleveland, Dallas, Houston, Los Angeles, and Chicago reported murder rates above the national average?

It is difficult to resist the suspicion that many of these differences result from the absence of consistent, standardized methods of ascertainment and reporting. Unfortunately, therefore, comparisons between different parts of the country, which might help

in the evaluation of causal factors, preventive efforts, and programs of rehabilitation, are too uncertain for confident conclusions.

It should be noted, however, that uncertainties involved in comparing crime rates at different times and between different localities are similar to those involved in studies of many social, psychological, and medical problems. Whether one is interested in
alcoholism, suicide, homosexuality, venereal disease, abortion, the
battered child, or a number of other conditions, it is difficult, and
perhaps impossible, to make reliable comparisons between different periods of time and between different societies or communi-
ties. It is surprising and discouraging to see how much variation
exists even today in the ascertainment of cases of all of the above
conditions. An unwary reader may easily be impressed with
three-, four-, even tenfold, differences in reported rates, and not
realize that all or most of the differences may be the result of
different ways of defining or ascertaining a case instead of actual
differences in incidence or prevalence. Too often, speculation
about the cause of an apparent difference may be encouraged
when no significant difference actually exists.

In addition to difficulties related to comparative crime statistics,
another important source of confusion in public understanding of
the nature and extent of the crime problem is the range and
variety of identified crime (61, 80). Crimes of violence (criminal
homicide, forcible rape, robbery, and aggravated assault) and
burglary, those crimes that evoke the greatest fear and concern
in the general public, make up a relatively small proportion of
reported crime, perhaps between 10 and 15 percent. On the other
hand, drunkenness, liquor law violations, disorderly conduct, vagrancy, prostitution and commercialized vice, gambling, juvenile
runaway, and curfew or loitering violations probably make up
about 50 percent or more of reported crime. These data suggest
that much, probably most, reported crime includes behavior that
the public may disapprove of but probably does not view with
fear and alarm.

Easy generalizations about crime that do not take into consideration these difficulties in interpreting the available data may

well lead to false explanations and solutions that are not valid. Furthermore, the fears that these generalizations can inspire may be an appropriate reaction to crimes of violence or burglary but not to the majority of reported crime.

No discussion of the crime problem in the United States can ignore racial and economic factors. The question of "white collar crime" will be discussed in a later chapter, but other crimes seem clearly to be committed proportionately more frequently by poor people and by members of disadvantaged minority groups, particularly blacks. What isn't so well appreciated, however, is that poor people and blacks are also disproportionately victimized (61, 80).

Compared to whites, non-whites are approximately eight to ten times more likely to be murdered, four times more likely to be raped, three-and-a-half times more likely to be robbed, and twice as likely to be assaulted. Only with regard to larceny are whites more likely to be victimized. Similar victimization patterns are seen in people with low incomes compared to those with high incomes; only with regard to larceny and auto theft are high income individuals at greater risk.

Finally, the limited available data indicate that in many cases, perhaps in most, homicide, aggravated assault, and forcible rape do not involve strangers. These crimes very often are committed by a spouse, relative, neighbor, friend, or acquaintance of the victim (80).

But even with regard to such socioeconomic, racial, and interpersonal aspects of crime, the data must be evaluated cautiously. The above patterns may be changing and may not be characteristic of all parts of the country. It is truly disturbing to be so uncertain about these basic epidemiologic considerations.

Still, it is clear that the United States has too much crime, especially violent crime against persons and burglary. We may not know how rapidly crime rates are changing or how much difference exists between social strata and geographic areas, but we do know that many hundreds of thousands of Americans are murdered, raped, assaulted, robbed, or burglarized each year— and that is too many for complacency.

TWO

Psychiatric Illness and the Medical Model

Crime and concern about it are not new. Societies have always been confronted by individuals who are unable or unwilling to conform to the law. And people have long pondered the significance of this nonconformity. The connection between psychiatric illness and criminal behavior has been of interest to physicians, lawyers, and theologians for many centuries. This interest has had two components: a desire to understand the nature of criminality, and the need to define the limits of criminal responsibility. These concerns pose difficulties because they raise questions about the meaning and definition of psychiatric illness. Are all cases of delinquency and crime manifestations of psychiatric disorders, or can it be established that psychiatric disturbances characterize only some criminals and not others?

An adequate discussion of psychiatric illness and criminality first requires defining and understanding the general nature of psychiatric illness. Psychiatry, a branch of medicine, is concerned with the study and treatment of various forms of psychopathology. These include disturbances of thinking, emotion, motivation, perception, learning, memory, maturation, and behavior. Such psychological disorders may be seen in a variety of combinations.

These combinations, in turn, may result from different causes, though, as yet, relatively little is known about the etiology of the most frequently encountered psychiatric conditions.

Patients may present with confusion, bizarre ideas, nervousness, anxiety, depression, hallucinations, compulsions, phobias, impaired memory, excessive use of alcohol or other drugs, slow learning, apathy, hostility, aggressive behavior, and many other complaints. These manifestations of mental or psychological disturbance may begin in childhood, adolescence, early adulthood, or later in life. Sometimes they occur in circumscribed episodes; at other times they persist as chronic or lifelong problems. They may be mild, causing only slight handicap, or they may be severe, leading to great disability and even death.

For some investigators the various combinations and permutations of symptoms, age of onset, patterns of illness through time, and severity are simply manifestations of a general propensity to psychiatric disorder. The particular combination in a given patient is of secondary importance, to be explained in terms of individual circumstances and idiosyncrasies. Treatment is directed primarily against the presumed general propensity to psychopathology.

For others, the particular combination of symptoms, onset, course, and severity is the key to ultimate understanding and control. This approach assumes that there are different psychiatric illnesses, just as there are different medical illnesses, and that the differences are reflected in different clinical patterns. Furthermore, it is assumed that different illnesses are the result of different causes and will respond to different treatments. This is what is meant by the medical or disease model in psychiatry.

The medical model ultimately requires a valid classification of psychiatric conditions. A valid classification of illness implies the ability to predict. The goal is a classification of illness in which each category is homogeneous, meaning that the cases demonstrate a uniform clinical picture and course, a predictable response to treatment, a common etiology and pathogenesis, and similar epidemiologic characteristics. Epidemiologic characteristics include methods of ascertainment (whether by coming to physicians complaining of symptoms, by coming for a regular check-up, or by population survey), social and economic status, familial patterns of illness (whether or not close relatives are sick with the same or related disorders), race, age, sex, marital status, and many others. In medicine, the term for classification is diagnosis, and physicians have always been concerned with diagnosis.

General principles and purposes of classification in a variety of scientific and scholarly pursuits have recently been discussed by R. R. Sokal (92). It may be helpful to review some of his ideas before proceeding to a fuller consideration of classification in medicine and psychiatry. He defines classification "as the ordering or arrangement of objects in groups or sets on the basis of their relationships. These relationships can be based on observable or inferred properties." He points out that "all classifications aim to achieve economy of memory. The world is full of single cases: single individuals of animal or plant species, single case histories of disease, single books, rocks, or industrial concerns. By grouping numerous individual objects into a taxon, the description of the taxon subsumes the individual descriptions of the objects contained within it." A taxon is "a set of objects of any rank recognized as a group in a classificatory system." Taxonomy refers to "the theoretical study of classification including its bases, principles, procedures, and rules."

Sokal continues:

. . . another purpose of classification is ease of manipulation. The objects are arranged in systems (that may or may not be hierarchic) in which the several taxa can be easily named and related to each other. . . . Ease of retrieval of information from a classificatory system is also a criterion frequently considered desirable.

The paramount purpose of a classification is to describe the structure and relationship of the constituent objects to each other and to similar objects, and to simplify these relationships in such a way that general statements can be made about classes of objects. The definition, description, and simplification of taxonomic structure is a challenging task. It is easy to perceive structure when it is obvious and discontinuous. Disjoint clusters separated by large empty regions are unambiguous. Thus horseshoe crabs or ginkgo trees are

unique species quite different from their nearest relatives. . . .
Much of what we observe in nature changes continuously in one or
another characteristic, but not necessarily with equally steep gra-
dients for each characteristic. Where should boundaries be drawn
in such cases? Must classification be a drawing of boundaries?
Would an adequate description and summarization of the continuity
of the objects be preferable to artificially erected boundaries? Uniform continuous change is, of course, not very frequent in nature.
Centripetal forces frequently hold together a certain structure over
a given domain and loosen their control only at zones of rapid in-
tergradation. . . .

Classifications that describe relationships among objects in nature
should generate hypotheses. In fact the principal scientific justifica-
tion for establishing classifications is that they are heuristic (in the
traditional meaning of this term as "stimulating interest as a means
of furthering investigation") and that they lead to the stating of a
hypothesis which can then be tested. . . .

Sokal then proceeds to discuss the distinction between monothetic and polythetic classifications, referring to the earlier work
by Beckner (5). He defines monothetic classification as

those in which the classes established differ by at least one property
which is uniform among the members of each class. Such classifications are especially useful in setting up taxonomic keys and certain
types of reference and filing systems.

In polythetic classifications, taxa are groups of individuals or objects that share a large proportion of their properties but do not
necessarily agree in any one property. Adoption of polythetic principles of classification negates the concept of an essence or type of
any taxon. No single uniform property is required for the definition
of a given group nor will any combination of characteristics necessarily define it. This somewhat disturbing concept is readily apparent when almost any class of objects is examined. Thus it is ex-
tremely difficult to define class attributes for such taxa as cows or
chairs. Although cows can be described as animals with four legs
that give milk, a cow that only has three legs and does not give milk
will still be recognized as a cow. Conversely there are other animals
with four legs that give milk that are not cows. It is similarly difficult to find necessary properties of the class "chairs." Properties that

might commonly be found in any chair may be missing in any given piece of furniture that would clearly be recognized as a chair. These somewhat contrived examples can be bolstered by numerous instances of classification ranging from archeology to zoology. When viewed from a historical perspective we find remarkable parallels in the gradual rejection of the type concept and the adoption of polythetic criteria in these various disciplines.

A corollary of polythetic classification is the requirement that many properties (characters) be used to classify objects. This is true of almost any type of object being classified. . . . Initial classifications based on few characters usually have had to be modified once information on additional characteristics was acquired. Diseases not differentiated in earlier times now represent separate clinical entities with the accumulation of new knowledge. . . .

Classifications based on many properties will be general; they are unlikely to be optimal for any single purpose, but might be useful for a great variety of purposes. . . .*

It will be seen that the diagnostic classification used in the studies to be described here—like those generally used in medicine—is polythetic. There are few pathognomonic features in medical diagnosis; the same symptom or sign may be seen in a number of different illnesses. From this observation arises the notion of differential diagnosis. For each prominent or striking feature of the history or physical examination, a number of diagnoses must be considered and then systematically eliminated until the correct diagnosis is established by confirmatory observations, x-rays, or laboratory tests.

Diagnosis has occupied a central role in medical thinking and practice for good reasons. Communication between physicians about their clinical experiences, education of new physicians, and evaluation and comparison of different treatments all require a uniform, valid, generally accepted diagnostic classification. Without it, medical thought and practice would be chaotic. There is no way to know we are talking or thinking about the same kinds

* Quotations from Science 185: 1115-1123, 1974, copyright 1974 by The American Association for the Advancement of Science. Reprinted by permission.

of patients without diagnosis. There is no way to educate and train new physicians without being able to organize and present knowledge in a systematic way based upon a diagnostic classification. There is no way to compare treatments unless they are applied to similar cases.

Patients also set great value on diagnosis. A patient consulting a physician because of illness has a number of questions, either explicit and direct or implicit and indirect. "What's wrong with me?" "What can I expect further in the way of symptoms and disability?" "Will I get well?" "How long will it take?" "If I recover, will I get sick again?" "If I don't get well, what can I expect in the way of persistent symptoms and disability?" "What difference will treatment make?"

Patients want to have names for their illnesses because they assume that the physician understands their cases when he can name their illnesses. They expect the physician to answer many of the above questions and so provide predictions about the future. Traditionally and logically, diagnosis and prognosis go together. The following quotation from Hippocrates (58) indicates how well he appreciated the importance of being able to predict what will happen to the patient.

> It appears to me a most excellent thing for the physician to cultivate Prognosis; for by foreseeing and foretelling in the presence of the sick, the present, the past, and the future, and explaining the omissions which patients have been guilty of, he will be the more readily believed to be acquainted with the circumstances of the sick; so that men will have confidence to entrust themselves to such a physician. And he will manage to cure best who has foreseen what is to happen from the present state of matters. For it is impossible to make all the sick well; this, indeed, would have been better than to be able to foretell what is going to happen; but since men die, some even before calling the physician, from violence of the disease, and some die immediately after calling him, having lived, perhaps, only one day or a little longer, and before the physician could bring his art to counteract the disease; it therefore becomes necessary to know the nature of such affections, how far they are above the power of the constitution; and, moreover, if there be anything divine in the dis-

eases, and to learn a foreknowledge of this also. Thus a man will be the more esteemed to be a good physician, for he will be the better able to treat those aright who can be saved, from having long anticipated everything; and by seeing and announcing beforehand those who will live and those who will die, he will thus escape censure.

Thus, for over 2500 years, the ability to predict correctly the course and outcome of illness has been a principal medical goal.

Scientific medicine has two major dimensions. One is the effort to explain clinical disease manifestations in terms of cellular and molecular processes. The other is the attempt to account for clinical manifestations and their course as functions of geographic, climatic, social, economic, familial, and therapeutic factors. The second goal requires follow-up studies. Careful description and systematic study of patients, assignment of patients to appropriate categories according to specific criteria, and repeated examinations over time are the essential activities in such research. The aim is to recognize, define, and measure factors that predispose to different illnesses and influence their severity, course, response to treatment, and outcome.

There should be no argument about the need for valid diagnoses. Some, however, resist the idea that diagnosis is essential because they do not recognize that diagnosis is simply the medical term for the classification of illness, and, while they might acknowledge the need for classification, they reject the medical or disease model in psychiatric conditions.

With the flowering of laboratory methods in general medicine, classification is based, where possible, primarily upon laboratory findings: culturing specific microorganisms, measuring various constituents of blood or spinal fluid, and recognizing certain changes in tissue biopsies or analyses. With such laboratory-defined groups, subclassifications based upon clinical and epidemiological characteristics are then possible. An analysis of symptoms, signs, clinical history, and certain epidemiological characteristics permits the classification of patients with many different disorders, including different cancers and heart disease, into subgroups having different prognoses and showing different responses to treatment (24-28, 41). Because of the reliability and consistency of laboratory methods, disease classification and nomenclature based upon them generally prevail. The clinical and epidemiological subclassification is often not considered a diagnosis, though it really is just that.

Consistent and reliable laboratory methods are not yet available in psychiatry. Classification is thus based directly upon clinical and epidemiological features; these classifications constitute the diagnoses. Precision and reliability of diagnosis, and thus ability to predict course, outcome, and response to treatment, are more limited in the absence of pertinent laboratory studies. Follow-up studies, by testing and refining the predictive value of diagnoses, often leading to revisions in diagnostic groupings, are essential for the development of a valid classification of illness. Diagnosis and prognosis are inseparable.

A natural question concerning psychiatric diagnosis is "What difference does it make?" Is this preoccupation merely academic, with little practical significance? It makes an important difference whether an illness is duodenal ulcer, gastric cancer, or ulcerative colitis. The situation is the same in the case of psychiatric illness. Even with the limitations of present-day diagnostic classification, important differences are evident. The life course, prognosis, complications, and response to treatment are quite different between anxiety neurosis and schizophrenia, hysteria and depression, or schizophrenia and mania. The risk of severe chronic disability, psychiatric hospitalization, suicide, and economic dependence will be quite different in each illness. Familial psychopathology and response to different treatments will likewise vary greatly from one diagnostic category to another (103).

Resistance to the disease model in psychiatry derives from a number of sources, but one of the most frequent and significant arguments is based on the assumption that the model presumes an "organic" etiology, meaning physical or chemical events as causes rather than social or psychologically significant events as causes. Since the causes of most common psychiatric conditions are unknown, opponents of the disease model reject it on the grounds that it prejudges the outcome of future research. If the medical or disease model required any such assumptions concerning cause, its opponents would be fully justified. But it does not. The disease model obviously is derived from general medical tradition and practice. It is appropriate then to review the way in which the disease model is used in general medicine before considering its appropriateness for psychiatry. The first point to note is that, by and large, psychiatrists are the only physicians concerned with the definition of disease. Other physicians have used the word for centuries without bothering to define it (42). The word was first used in the fourteenth century and was derived from Anglo-Norman (disese, desese) and Old French (desaise, desayse) (75). Throughout its history, it has been used very generally. The following quotations from a number of dictionaries present a cross section of definitions. *Webster's New Collegiate Dictionary,* 7th edition, defines disease as "an impairment of the normal state of the living animal or plant body that affects the performance of the vital functions." It offers "sickness" as an alternate definition. *Dorland's Medical Dictionary,* 24th edition, defines it as "a definite morbid process having a characteristic train of symptoms; it may affect the whole body or any of its parts, and its etiology, pathology, and prognosis may be known or unknown." *Stedman's Medical Dictionary,* 20th edition, defines it as "Morbus; illness; sickness; an interruption or perversion of function of any of the organs; a morbid change in any of the tissues, or an abnormal state of the body as a whole, continuing for a longer or shorter period." And finally, *Webster's Dictionary of Synonyms* offers the following synonyms: affection, ailment, malady, complaint, and distemper.

These definitions indicate that disease, illness, and sickness are equivalent terms referring to a wide range of conditions, leading to the conclusion "that any condition associated with discomfort, pain, disability, death, or an increased liability to these states, *regarded by physicians and the public as properly the responsibility of the medical profession,* may be considered a disease" (41).

Formal definitions of disease are avoided by most physicians, and those offered by dictionaries are very general and hence not

21

helpful. An understanding of the disease or medical model may be obtained by examining the way physicians approach general medical problems. For example, discussions in standard textbooks are divided into definition, diagnostic criteria, differential diagnosis, epidemiology, etiology, pathogenesis, treatment, prognosis, and so forth.

Believing that there are different illnesses and recognizing that individual patients may vary in their manifestations of a particular disease, physicians try to distinguish between features that are clearly the result of the illness under consideration and those that may represent idiosyncrasies of the individual patient or his circumstances. The basic assumption is that when a patient is sick, the nature of the illness, reflected in the diagnosis, is the most important clue to understanding and management. Consideration of other features, including epidemiology, etiology, pathogenesis, and treatment, are based upon the specific illness involved. This, then, is how the medical model operates when it is applied to nonpsychiatric illnesses; the same operations are applicable to psychiatric illnesses.

The relationship between biology and psychiatric disorders is also involved in thinking about the medical model and psychiatric disorders. Medicine is, to a major degree, applied human biology. Rapid advances in biology during recent decades have already had profound effects on general medicine. It seems inevitable that this trend will continue and will similarly influence psychiatry. Advances in genetics, developmental biology, and neurobiology cannot help but shape psychiatric thinking and practice. In fact, it is highly likely that biological knowledge and insight will increasingly influence the social sciences, philosophy, and the humanities as well. Studies of man in which his biological nature is ignored cannot lead to full understanding. The profound consequences of culture, economic forces, climatic and geographic variations, nutrition, and a wide range of other environmental influences can be understood completely only if biological variation is studied simultaneously. While the place of biology in general medicine is accepted, its place in psychiatry is still controversial. Some of the resistance to the medical model in psychiatry is based upon an unwillingness to accept the importance of biology in understanding psychiatric conditions.

Psychiatric Studies of Crime

Psychiatric investigations of criminals have generally suffered from psychiatric bias in the selection of subjects and from the absence of specific diagnostic criteria. An additional important limitation has been the absence of psychiatric follow-up and family studies to validate the psychiatric diagnoses and evaluations. Without these, and without specific diagnostic criteria, firm conclusions from these investigations cannot be drawn with confidence.

Representative publications in English will be summarized in Chapter 6. It is not possible to carry out any large-scale clinical study without important methodological deficiencies. But the repeated failure to provide diagnostic criteria, and the total absence of psychiatric follow-up and family studies make all of these reports incomplete. These omissions pointed the way to the present investigation.

THREE
Design of the Study

Selection of Subjects

No aspect of human research is more important than selecting the subjects to be studied. The investigator should maximize the likelihood that his results and conclusions will have general applicability. If his sample does not truly represent the universe he is studying, his efforts may be largely wasted.

The study of criminal behavior presents special problems in this regard. Not everyone who commits an illegal act is apprehended. Some who are apprehended are not tried, others are not convicted, and not everyone who is convicted is guilty. Thus, it is impossible to select a completely satisfactory sample.

Whether criminals who are caught differ from those who escape detection cannot be settled even though it is a vital question directly bearing on the results and conclusions of any study. It is plausible to suspect that there may be significant differences in age, race, education, intelligence, motivation, judgment, and psychopathology between apprehended and nonapprehended criminals. Similar differences may exist between those tried and not tried and between those convicted and not convicted.

The way to deal with these issues is to study groups of subjects selected in different ways and at different times: population surveys of criminal behavior (whether or not apprehended), samples chosen at the time of arrest, before trial, after trial, after sentencing, and so forth. Each method presents special problems, however. People are understandably reluctant to admit and discuss criminal behavior, particularly if they have not been caught, so the investigator can never be certain of the subject's full cooperation. Attempts to study subjects at the time of arrest or before trial would encounter resistance from some attorneys and judges and might be handicapped by the reluctance of the accused to be candid for fear of jeopardizing his legal chances. The investigator might be compelled to testify at the trial, thus limiting any assurances he could make concerning confidentiality, without which many subjects would refuse to cooperate.

After trial, guilty subjects who had escaped conviction might be cautious about participating in any study, and, until possible appeals had been carried out, convicted subjects and their attorneys might similarly shun such study.

Finally, if the study is to include long-term follow-up to confirm and validate psychiatric diagnosis and to observe criminal recidivism, social adjustment, and life style, and relate these to psychiatric diagnosis, subjects cannot be selected at the time of sentencing. Great variability in the length of sentence, determined by the judge, nature of the crime, history of previous conviction, age, sex, race, and other circumstances, would make a reasonable follow-up study impossible. Subjects might be sentenced to serve from one to 20 years. Some would be paroled after serving part of the full sentence; others would be required to spend the entire time in prison. At any follow-up period, subjects would vary greatly in the amount of time out of prison and exposed to the risk of recidivism.

Thus, despite many reservations, a systematic psychiatric study of criminality, if it is to include personal follow-up, must be based, at least in part, on a sample of convicted criminals who are all studied at the same time before return to the community. Furthermore, the subjects must be selected without any psychiatric bias; they must not be identified because of suspected or known psychiatric disorders. Finally, since nearly any method of selecting subjects may result in some systematic bias related to the goals of the study, such possible bias must be recognized, assessed, and, if possible, corrected for.

Why Study Felons?

Crime is usually divided into two broad categories: misdemeanors and felonies. Misdemeanors comprise the less serious minor crimes; felonies, the more serious major crimes. The crimes of greatest concern to the public—such as murder, rape, robbery, burglary, aggravated assault, grand larceny, and auto theft—are felonies. They are the crimes included in the Uniform Crime Reports of the FBI. Because the public is most concerned about felonies, including crimes of violence, we decided to study this category of crime.

Selection of Male Felons

With the help and cooperation of the Missouri Board of Probation and Parole, we studied 223 consecutive male felons, including "parolees" and "flat-timers." A parolee is an individual who, because of his record and prison behavior, is discharged before completing his sentence, to be followed and supervised by a parole officer; a flat-timer is an individual who, also because of his previous record and prison behavior, is passed over for parole and is required to serve the full sentence, with no obligation to undergo parole office supervision after discharge from prison. Both categories of felons were included in order to study a wide spectrum of criminals.

The parolees were selected by taking every new male case assigned to the St. Louis Office of Probation and Parole between November 1, 1959 and April 30, 1960. There were 129 such men: 47 were referred directly from a Missouri court to the Office of Probation and Parole, 26 were referred from the Missouri intermediate reformatory, and 56 were referred from the Missouri State prison. Four of the prison parolees were not examined because they broke parole within 24 hours and were either returned to prison or were being hunted by the police. One prison parolee refused to cooperate with the study. One reformatory parolee and one parolee referred directly from the courts managed to avoid study but did not directly refuse.

The flat-timers were selected by taking, from a given target date, approximately the next 50 men who would be eligible for discharge from the prison and from the intermediate reformatory. These men had already been denied parole and were expected to be discharged within several months. The men were chosen consecutively, beginning with the man who would be discharged soonest. At the prison, 50 consecutive men were assigned for study; however, only 49 were examined because one was placed in solitary confinement for infraction of rules, and the warden would not permit him to be released for study. At the intermediate reformatory, 53 consecutive men were assigned, and all were examined. Out of a total of 231 possible parolees and flat-timers, 223, or 96 percent, were examined.

When each man was assigned to the local Probation and Parole office, he was told that it was now part of the routine procedure in the office to obtain a psychiatric evaluation of each parolee. An appointment was made for the man to come to our hospital for an interview. At the beginning of the interview, the subject was told that the psychiatric evaluation was routine and that the individual was not selected because psychiatric illness was suspected. He was told that the parole office had made available to the psychiatrists the man's record but that the psychiatric material would be treated confidentially. The man was further told that the goal of the study was to learn more about factors associated with "getting into trouble with the law." The interviews were carried out in ordinary hospital offices. The flat-timers were introduced to the psychiatric evaluation along similar lines. These interviews were carried out in offices assigned by the respective institutions.

Selection of Relatives of Male Felons

The study was limited to first-degree relatives living in the St. Louis area. The relatives were studied between October 1962 and October 1965. No first-degree relatives of 115 of the 223 men in the original sample could be located in the St. Louis area. The available records for 91 of these men suggested that there were no first-degree relatives in the St. Louis area. Additional efforts in these cases plus 19 others failed to uncover any first-degree relatives living in the St. Louis area. For four of the original subjects, all the first-degree relatives were known to be dead. One of the original subjects had been adopted as an infant and knew nothing of his own family.

One or more first-degree relatives of 93 of the remaining 108 original subjects were interviewed. Of these 93 subjects, 68 were parolees and 25 were flat-timers. Since most of the flat-timers were not from the St. Louis area originally, it is not surprising that fewer of their relatives were able to be interviewed.

The families of the 93 men contained 519 first-degree relatives who were at least 15 years old at the time the relatives were studied or who had died after reaching their 15th birthday. It was possible to interview personally 260 of these relatives. The other 259 were not interviewed for the following reasons: dead, 64; not living in the St. Louis area, 112; not located, 43; refused or uncooperative, 40. Of those relatives who were alive and not geographically unavailable, 76 percent were interviewed.

As part of the family history elicited from interviewed relatives, information was obtained about all first-degree relatives of the person being interviewed. This information primarily concerned alcoholism, psychiatric hospitalization, schizophrenia, police trouble, suicide attempts, suicides, and sociopathy (see below). The data obtained during these interviews were used to supplement the findings obtained about interviewed relatives (see below).

Selection of Female Felons

All the female felons under supervision in District 8 of the Missouri State Board of Probation and Parole were selected for study:

71 women as of July 1, 1969, plus 7 new cases during July and August. This group included parolees from the Missouri State Prison for Women at Tipton and parolees from the St. Louis County courts plus a few interstate transfers. Very few women felons are required to serve the full sentence without parole, so subjects who were flat-timers were not included.

Interviews were arranged by the parole officer in charge of the case. The explanation given the women was similar to that given to the male felons. The interviews were usually carried out at the parole office. Because of transportation or other difficulties, the interview occasionally took place either in the subject's home or at the hospital. Each woman was told that the parole board would make its records available to the physicians but that everything she told the physicians would be kept entirely confidential.

Of the 78 possible subjects, 3 moved to other cities where they were to complete their parole periods, 2 absconded before study, 3 refused, and 4 repeatedly failed to keep appointments. This left 66 women, 90 percent of those remaining in St. Louis, who were interviewed.

Selection of Relatives of Female Felons

The families of the 66 index women included 288 first-degree relatives who were 18 years of age or older at the time the relatives were studied or who had died after reaching their 18th birthday. This included 132 parents, 131 siblings, and 25 children. Of these relatives, 106 were interviewed. The other 182 were not interviewed for the following reasons: dead, 48; not living within 50 miles of St. Louis, 104; identity unknown (fathers), 2; not located, 5; refusal by relative, 12; refusal by index subject, 11. Thus, 79 percent of known relatives who were alive and geographically available were interviewed.

Family history information was obtained from each index subject and interviewed relative. Diagnoses suspected from these data were based on the same criteria used for interviewed relatives (see below). Sociopathy was distinguished from alcoholism or drug dependence on the basis of a definite history of juvenile onset of antisocial behavior or repeated criminality in the absence of alcohol or drug abuse. The only other specific diagnoses attempted from the family history data were schizophrenia, homosexuality, primary affective disorder, and dementia. Differentiation between anxiety neurosis and hysteria was not attempted.

Information about relatives was also obtained from independent records. Parole records of the index subjects were reviewed for information about the relatives. Records of the State Board of Probation and Parole, which supervises felons, and of a local medium security jail, which holds those convicted of minor offenses, were reviewed for information about relatives. Medical information about relatives was obtained from general hospitals affiliated with Washington University, and particular attention was given to evidence of alcoholism. The records of affiliated psychiatric hospitals were also reviewed for information about both interviewed and noninterviewed relatives. Diagnoses from records were based on the same criteria that were used in the interview.

Selection of Wives of Convicted Male Felons

Of the 176 men interviewed at follow-up, 33 had never married, 21 were divorced, 21 were separated, one was a widower, and 100 were married and living with spouse. Wives of 109 of these men were interviewed. Eight wives refused the interview, the husband refused interview of the wife in 4 cases, 2 wives were dead (one following divorce from her husband), and 20 wives could not be located (all divorced or separated from their husbands). Thus, 77 percent of the current or most recent wives of the interviewed men, or 90 percent of the wives who were located alive, were interviewed. There were no interracial marriages: 81 percent of the 104 white wives and 64 percent of the 39 black wives were interviewed. Eighty-nine percent of the 100 married wives and 48 percent of the 42 divorced or separated wives were interviewed. Only 10 percent of the white men were currently divorced or separated compared to 52 percent of the black men (p<.001); this probably accounts for the racial difference in percent interviewed.

The current or most recent wife of 7 other index men, who were themselves not interviewed at follow-up, was also interviewed. These wives were all white. Four were divorced or separated, one was a widow, and 2 were married and living with their husbands. Thus, a total of 91 white and 25 black women were interviewed. Their mean age was 30.

Comparison Between Male and Female Felons

The studies of male and female felons were separated by several years. As a result, they were not identical in all respects, since certain observations were made in one study but not in the other. The differences were not great, however, and, as will be evident below, the major features of the two studies were the same.

Diagnostic Criteria

An appropriate psychiatric investigation of criminality requires specific diagnostic criteria, follow-up to test the consistency and validity of the diagnoses, and a study of close relatives to determine whether similar disorders are present. A provisionally valid diagnostic classification of psychiatric disorders is available, based on work by many investigators in different countries (23, 103). This classification is based primarily on follow-up and family studies, which indicate that, within limits, each diagnostic category is specific for clinical picture, natural history, and familial illness patterns. Additional work is still necessary, however, to refine the classification and so additional follow-up and family studies are desirable in any investigation of the association between psychiatric diagnosis and other variables. The investigations to be reported here, therefore, were designed to include follow-up studies and studies of first-degree relatives.

The same diagnostic criteria were used throughout, with some slight modifications noted below.

Anxiety Neurosis. The general definition of anxiety neurosis was taken from Wheeler *et al.* (99). Subjects were included in this category if they met one of the following criteria: (A) they presented a history of recurrent nervousness plus either dyspnea or palpitation; (B) they presented a history of both recurrent dyspnea and palpitation; or (C) they presented a history of recurrent anxiety attacks. In addition, such symptoms had to occur in the absence of exertion, overtly frightening experiences such as near accidents, or evidence of cardiac or chest disease. Anxiety symptoms in patients with hysteria, obsessional neurosis, schizophrenia, or primary affective disorder (see below) did not lead to a separate diagnosis of anxiety neurosis. Such symptoms in subjects with organic brain syndrome, alcoholism, drug dependence, sociopathy, or homosexuality (see below) did lead to an additional diagnosis of anxiety neurosis.

Hysteria (Briquet's Syndrome). The general definition of hysteria was taken from Purtell *et al.* (81). The specific criteria of Perley and Guze (76) were used. To receive a diagnosis, the following criteria had to be met. (A) The patient had to present a dramatic or complicated medical history beginning before the age of 35. (B) The patient had to report at least 25 of the following symptoms for a *definite* diagnosis and 20-24 for a *probable* diagnosis distributed among at least 9 of these 10 groups of symptoms: group 1—feeling sickly for most of life, headache; group 2—blindness, paralysis, anesthesia, aphonia, fits or convulsions, unconsciousness, amnesia, deafness, hallucinations, or urinary retention; group 3—fatigue, lump in the throat, fainting spells, visual blurring, weakness, or dysuria; group 4—breathing difficulty, palpitation, anxiety attacks, chest pain, or dizziness; group 5—anorexia, weight loss, marked fluctuations in weight, nausea, abdominal bloating, food intolerances, diarrhea, or constipation; group 6—abdominal pain or vomiting; group 7—dysmenorrhea, menstrual irregularity (including amenorrhea for at least two months), or excessive menstrual bleeding; group 8—sexual indifference, sexual frigidity, dyspareunia, other sexual difficulties, hospitalization for hyperemesis, gravidarum, or vomiting for all nine months of pregnancy; group 9—back pain, joint pain, extremity pain, burning pains of the sexual organs, mouth, or rectum, or other bodily pains; and group 10—nervousness, fears, depressed feelings, need to quit work or inability to carry on regular duties because of feeling sick, crying easily, feeling life was hopeless, thinking a good deal about dying, wanting to die, thinking of suicide, or suicide attempts. (C) No other diagnosis could be made to explain the symptoms.

This definition of hysteria is to be contrasted to that of *conversion symptoms* (40), a term used in a purely descriptive way to refer to unexplained symptoms suggesting neurological disease, of which the most common and classical examples (the so-called "pseudoneurological" symptoms) are listed in group two of the hysteria criteria.

Obsessional Neurosis. The diagnostic criteria were similar to those of Pollitt (78). In order to receive this diagnosis, a subject had to report an obsession, defined as a recurrent or persistent idea, thought, image, feeling, impulse, or movement, accompanied by a sense of subjective compulsion and a desire to resist it, the event being recognized by the individual as foreign to his personality or nature ("ego-alien"). An obsessional neurosis would be one in which such obsessional symptoms were the dominant feature of the case. Subjects with so-called obsessional personality patterns but without specific obsessions and subjects whose obsessions were secondary to schizophrenia or primary affective disorders would be excluded from this diagnostic group.

Schizophrenia. We followed Langfeldt (64) and Stephens *et al.* (94) in using this diagnosis to refer to a chronic, frequently progressive disorder characterized by an insidious onset, poor prepsychotic adjustment, prominent delusions or hallucinations, severe disability in interpersonal relationships and job performance, minimal if any affective symptoms, and a clear sensorium.

Primary Affective Disorders. We applied this diagnosis to all primary affective disorders (85). Only unipolar cases were seen

(103). The description of Cassidy *et al.* was followed (9). In order to receive this diagnosis a subject had to report (A) a mood change including any of the following: blue, worried, discouraged, depressed, anxious, low, scared, fearful, angry, afraid, gloomy, hopeless, despondent, "don't care," happy, empty, or disgusted; (B) at least six of the following ten symptoms: thinking slow, poor appetite, constipation, insomnia, feeling tired, loss of concentration, suicidal ideas, weight loss, decreased sex interest, or agitation manifested by wringing hands, pacing, press of complaints; (C) an episode of illness arising without pre-existing psychiatric difficulties or symptoms, except for previous episodes of depression or mania, e.g., without pre-existing anxiety neurosis, hysteria, alcoholism, schizophrenia, etc. If such pre-existing illnesses existed, the affective disturbance was considered to be secondary and the subject was grouped under the primary disorder.

Organic Brain Syndrome. Disorders characterized by evidence of significant memory impairment and disorientation were included under this diagnosis. Slight memory impairment in subjects over age 60 was ignored.

Alcoholism. The interview included questions about many of the symptoms of alcoholism that have been emphasized by Jellinek (60). In order to receive a diagnosis of alcoholism, symptoms in at least three of the following four groups were required. Group 1 included: (A) tremors or other manifestations of delirium tremens, or a history of cirrhosis; (B) impotence associated with drinking; (C) alcoholic "blackouts"; (D) alcoholic binges or benders. Group 2 included: (A) subject had not been able to stop drinking when he wanted to stop; (B) subject tried to control drinking by allowing himself to drink only under certain circumstances such as only after 5 p.m. or only on weekends, or only with other people; (C) drinking before breakfast; (D) drinking nonbeverage forms of alcohol. Group 3 included: (A) arrests for drinking; (B) traffic difficulties associated with drinking; (C) trouble at work because of drinking; (D) fighting associated with drinking.

Group 4 included: (A) subject felt he drank too much; (B) family objected to his drinking; (C) other people objected to his drinking; (D) he lost friends because of drinking; (E) he felt guilty about his drinking.

At first, the criteria for alcoholism included items concerning frequency and quantity of drinking (49). Further experience indicated that the reliability and validity of the data concerning frequency or quantity of drinking were hard to establish. In addition, it was found that these items could be omitted without affecting the diagnosis, so they were excluded from consideration in subsequent diagnoses of alcoholism.

A diagnosis of questionable alcoholism was made when there was a drinking problem, but the specific criteria for the diagnosis of alcoholism were not fulfilled: if a subject reported three or more symptoms but these were limited to two groups, for example, or if a subject reported such striking symptoms as binges and job troubles.

Drug Dependence

This diagnosis was used to include subjects who reported withdrawal symptoms, hospitalization for addiction, or recurrent and prolonged use of drugs. A diagnosis of questionable drug dependence was used when the history was uncertain but drug dependence was strongly suspected.

Sociopathy

This diagnosis was made if at least two of the following five manifestations were present in addition to a history of police trouble (other than traffic offenses): a history of excessive fighting (if under age 18, leading to trouble with adults; if 18 or older, fighting with a weapon or multiple fights), school delinquency (truancy, suspension, expulsion, trouble with principal), a poor job record (being fired, quitting a job without having another, or being unable to hold a job for a year), a period of wanderlust, or being a runaway. If any of the individual diagnostic criteria were scored as questionable, the subject received a diagnosis of questionable sociopathy. For women, a history of prostitution could be substituted for one of the 5 manifestations.

Homosexuality

This diagnosis was used for subjects who reported recurrent or persistent homosexual experiences. These would generally conform to Kinsey grades of 4 or higher.

Undiagnosed Disorders

If a subject was thought to be ill or reported a number of possible psychiatric symptoms and yet failed to fit into any of the above diagnostic categories, he was placed in the group of undiagnosed disorders.

Research Interviews

The interviews were conducted by trained psychiatrists or advanced psychiatric residents, all members of the Department of Psychiatry of Washington University School of Medicine. Each interviewer was familiar with the diagnostic criteria because, for many years, a significant element in the department's training program had been a concern with the development and validation of these diagnostic criteria.

Different psychiatrists participated in the various stages of the overall investigation so that those who conducted the index interviews of the male felons did not conduct the follow-up interviews and the interviews with wives. The follow-up and spouse interviews were conducted by psychiatrists who were familiar with the overall results of the index study but who did not consult the record of the index interview until after completing the follow-up interview and the interview with the wife. Interviews with the first-degree relatives of the male felons were conducted by still other psychiatrists. In this way, the interviews at any one stage of the study were not affected by the interviews at any other stage. On the other hand, the index study of female felons and the study of their first-degree relatives were conducted by the same psychiatrist, so that some contamination was possible. The same structured interview was used throughout these studies (Appendix A). It included a history of current and past illnesses and injuries; a description of all hospitalizations and operations; and a detailed symptom inventory designed to elicit the manifestations of anxiety neurosis, hysteria, obsessional neurosis, schizophrenia, primary affective disorder, organic brain syndrome, alcoholism, drug dependence, sociopathy, and homosexuality. In addition, a detailed family history of psychiatric difficulties and a history of parental home experiences were obtained. The interview also included sections dealing with school history, job history, marital history, military experiences, and police troubles. Specific inquiry was also made about suicide attempts. A mental status examination concluded the interview. Specific criteria were provided for scoring individual items. In general, these criteria selected symptoms or features that appeared to be medically significant because they required treatment or interfered with the subject's normal life.

Record Information

In all phases of this investigation, copies and abstracts of records were sought from hospitals, physicians, police, prison and parole authorities, the Federal Bureau of Investigation, and the Veterans' Administration. The extent and completeness of such records varied from one subject to another and from one study to another. Nevertheless, the records provided valuable data that helped us to evaluate and corroborate information obtained from the various interviews.

Bias in Selection of Subjects

The method of selecting felons permitted two loopholes through which certain categories of criminals might be lost: criminals sent directly from the courts to the state hospital for the criminally insane, and criminals kept permanently at the state hospital when sent for observation from the prison or intermediate reformatory. An analysis of the figures for 1959 and 1960, the years when the male felons were selected, indicated that approximately 1.5 percent of men convicted of a felony in the St. Louis area (city and county) were sent directly to the state hospital and less than one percent of the inmates of the intermediate reformatory and state prison were permanently transferred to the state hospital. Thus, approximately 2 percent of felons were missed through these channels. This will be considered further (Chapter 5) in the description of an attempt to correct partly for this omission.

There is another way in which psychiatrically ill offenders may escape identification in a study of criminals. An unknown percentage of such individuals, apprehended after committing criminal acts, are removed from the criminal justice system through decisions by police officers, prosecutors, or judges. These officials may avoid or dismiss criminal charges and either recommend (in less serious cases) or require (in more serious cases) psychiatric care. Instead of going through arrest, prosecution, and trial, such individuals may be referred to psychiatric clinics or committed to psychiatric hospitals via civil commitment. Presumably these actions are more likely when the apprehended criminal is overtly and strikingly psychiatrically ill, particularly with florid symptoms such as delusions, hallucinations, grossly impaired memory, or marked disorientation. Unfortunately, no data are available about the frequency of such actions, and it is therefore not possible to estimate accurately their effect on studies such as those to be described below. But informal opinion suggests that only a very small percentage of apprehended criminals in Missouri are handled this way. Recently, in a few localities, systematic programs have been initiated to divert selected offenders from the criminal justice system as part of renewed efforts at rehabilitation (104).

FOUR
Male Felons

INDEX STUDY (49)

Age, Race, and Education

When originally studied, the average age of the 223 convicted male felons was between 27 and 28, with a range of 15 to 78. Their median age was between 23 and 24. Fifty-nine men were under age 20; 95 were in their twenties; 39 in their thirties; 15 in their forties; 8 in their fifties; 5 in their sixties; and 2 in their seventies. Thus, only 13 percent were at least 40 years old, and nearly 70 percent were less than 30. No striking difference was seen between parolees and flat-timers.

Sixty of the men (27 percent) were black. They averaged 2 years older than the 163 white felons.

The men had completed an average of 8.5 years of school. Twenty-three (10 percent) had graduated from high school. Five (2 percent) had attended one or more years of college, but none had graduated from college. There was no racial difference in years of school completed, percent graduated from high school, or percent with education beyond high school. Forty-six percent had failed one or more grades, 3 percent were illiterate (2 percent of the white felons and 7 percent of the black felons); another 15 percent were poor readers as judged by their ability to read a newspaper aloud (13 percent of the white felons and 20 percent of the black felons). Over half (52 percent) had been repeatedly truant. More than a third (37 percent) had been involved in repeated fights in school leading to difficulties with school authorities. And a third (32 percent) had been suspended or expelled from school at least once.

Job, Marriage, and Military Experiences

A poor work record was found in a substantial number. A third of those out of school or jail in the two years before the index conviction had had three or more jobs. More than a third had never held a job for as long as a year, and nearly a third had been fired one or more times.

Forty-five percent had been married at least once, and nearly half of these (48 percent) had been divorced at least once.

Eighty-five men had seen military service. Half of these had received a disciplinary discharge, and another 10 percent had received a medical discharge, leaving 40 percent with an honorable discharge. Nearly half of those who had been in military service (48 percent) had gone AWOL, 44 percent had been court-martialed, and more than a third had been demoted or fined.

Social Background

About 40 percent of the men were born in the St. Louis metropolitan area, another 15 percent came from other metropolitan areas, and the rest, about 45 percent, came from rural areas, small towns, and cities whose population was under 50,000. More than a third of the men were "on their own" before age 17, and more than half before age 18. About 70 percent of their fathers had unskilled or semi-skilled occupations, Otis-Dudley-Duncan job classifications less than 20 (84).

Parental Home Experience

Gross disruption or disturbance of the family home was reported by the great majority of the male felons. Ten percent of their mothers and 14 percent of their fathers had died before the index subject had reached age 15. Three percent of their mothers and 6 percent of their fathers had deserted their families. Forty percent of the parents' marriages had been terminated by divorce or permanent separation. Twenty-nine percent of the fathers were reported to be alcoholics and 18 percent had been jailed; altogether, a third of the fathers were reported as having been alcoholic or jailed. Among the mothers, 4 percent were reported to be alcoholics, but only one mother had been jailed. Thirty percent of the felons had had to live with relatives or friends or in foster homes or orphanages.

Nearly two-thirds of the men experienced during their childhood or adolescence parental death, desertion, divorce or separation, alcoholism, or criminality.

History of Previous Delinquency and Crime

Excessive fighting was reported by 64 percent of the men. Nearly half, 47 percent, continued to fight after adulthood. More than a third, 35 percent, reported having run away from home overnight during childhood at least once. Over a fourth, 26 percent, reported periods of wanderlust during which they wandered aimlessly over the country without any plans or regular jobs. Only 10 percent of the men had never been arrested prior to the index crime. Nearly two-thirds, 63 percent, had been arrested 4 or more times; a third, 33 percent, had been arrested 10 or more times. Twenty-nine percent had served a period in reform school, and 54 percent had previously been in prison.

Index Crimes

The 223 men had been convicted of 239 felonies as index offenses (Table 1). The most frequent was burglary, seen in over 40 per-

TABLE 1
INDEX CRIMES: MALE FELONS (49)

Burglary	92
Larceny	48
Robbery	32
Auto Theft	19
Check Forgery	18
Homicide*	15
Rape†	11
Sex Offenses	4
	239‡

* Including 4 attempted homicides.
† Including 5 attempted rapes and 3 statutory rapes.
‡ Some men convicted of more than one crime.

cent. Crimes against persons (rape, homicide, and robbery) were the index crimes in over 26 percent.

Psychiatric Diagnoses

Sociopathy. The great majority had an early onset of delinquency, associated with frequent school difficulties, frequent fights, a poor job history, poor marital adjustment, frequent wanderlust, a bad military history with recurrent troubles, excessive drinking and drug use, and recurrent trouble with the police. Seventy-eight percent met the criteria for sociopathy.

Alcoholism. Problems associated with drinking were very common. Well over half of the subjects (121) reported one or more of the problems associated with drinking described in Chapter 3. These men reported a mean of 6.2 alcoholism symptoms. Ninety-six men, 43 percent, fulfilled the criteria for the diagnosis of alcoholism. These men reported an average of 7.2 diagnostic alcoholism symptoms. The other 25 subjects were considered questionable alcoholics. Seventeen men, 8 percent, were lifelong abstainers. This was associated with race since nine of the teetotalers, 54 percent, were black.

Anxiety Neurosis. Twenty-six men, 12 percent, fulfilled the diagnostic criteria for anxiety neurosis. Sixteen of these 26 men were alcoholics. Anxiety neurosis was present in 17 percent of the 96 alcoholics and in 9 percent of the 102 nonalcoholics. One anxiety neurotic was a questionable alcoholic. The difference between the alcoholics and nonalcoholics, while suggestive, was not statistically significant.

In addition to the 16 alcoholics and one questionable alcoholic, one anxiety neurotic was drug dependent. Eight of the anxiety neurotics were neither alcoholics nor drug dependent. Four of these were sociopaths without other clinical diagnoses; the other four fell into no other clinical category.

Drug Dependence. Thirty-four men, 15 percent, had used or experimented with illicit drugs. Twenty-four men, 10 percent, had used drugs only occasionally and were not considered to have had any complications from this experimentation. The other 10 men, 5 percent of the entire sample, reported withdrawal symptoms, hospitalization for addiction, or recurrent and prolonged use of drugs, and thus met the diagnostic criteria. Four of these 10 men were also alcoholics.

Schizophrenia. Two subjects, one percent, met the diagnostic criteria for schizophrenia. One was also an alcoholic, but his schizophrenic symptoms began many years before the heavy drinking.

Homosexuality. Eighteen men, 8 percent, reported some overt homosexual experience. Four men, 2 percent, indicated that homosexuality was limited to the time in prison. Three men, or about one percent, gave a history of recurrent and persistent homosexuality, and one of them had been convicted of homosexual relations with a minor. These three men were regarded as significantly homosexual. The other 15 reported only occasional and isolated homosexual experiences and were, therefore, not diagnosed as homosexual. None of the subjects reported exclusively homosexual experiences.

Epilepsy. Recurrent, typical grand mal convulsions were reported by three men, about one percent of the sample. One man was an alcoholic; the other two received no additional psychiatric diagnoses.

Mental Deficiency. Intellectual function was estimated clinically on the basis of the school history and mental status examination. Sixteen men, 7 percent, were thought to be below normal in intelligence. The results of psychometric examination were available in the records of three of these men; they had IQ's in the 80 to 85 range. Only one man was considered to have a degree of intellectual impairment sufficiently great to preclude a normal self-sufficient life in the community. He was sent to the St. Louis State Training School at the time of discharge from prison.

Clinical evaluation of intelligence is useful only for gross estimates. In the absence of uniform psychometric examination, the findings must be regarded as tentative. Most investigators agree, however, that the average intelligence of criminals is only slightly lower than the average intelligence of controls, and that severe mental deficiency is present in only a small percentage of criminals, even though it may be present in a higher percentage of criminals than of the general population.

Brain Syndrome. One man met the criteria for chronic brain syndrome. He was an alcoholic of long standing.

Undiagnosed. One man had a chronic psychiatric disorder that failed to meet the criteria of any defined psychiatric condition. He was neither an alcoholic nor drug dependent.

To summarize: only 23 men, or 10 percent, failed to receive one or more psychiatric diagnoses. Another 9 men, or 4 percent, received some psychiatric diagnosis but not sociopathy, alcoholism, or drug dependence. All the others, over 85 percent, received one or more of these 3 diagnoses, whether or not they received other diagnoses as well (Table 2).

TABLE 2
PSYCHIATRIC DIAGNOSES AT INDEX STUDY OF MALE
FELONS (49)

	%
Sociopathy (Antisocial Personality)	78
Alcoholism	
Definite	43
Questionable	11
Anxiety Neurosis	12
Drug Dependence	5
Schizophrenia	1
Homosexuality	1
Epilepsy	1
Mental Deficiency	<1
Brain Syndrome	<1
Undiagnosed	<1
Any Psychiatric Diagnosis	90
Sociopathy, Alcoholism, or Drug Dependence	85

History of Suicide Attempts, Injuries, and Hospitalizations

Eleven men, 5 percent, reported a previous suicide attempt. Nine
were alcoholics, one was drug dependent, and one was a questionable alcoholic.

Sixty-seven men, 30 percent, reported a total of 90 hospitalizations for treatment of serious injuries, the result of accidents or
fights. Seventy-eight men, 35 percent, reported lesser injuries re-
quiring medical attention outside of hospitals.

Fifteen men, 7 percent, reported a total of 30 psychiatric hospitalizations, some for attempted suicide, some for drug or alcohol abuse, and some for observation.

Altogether, about 85 percent of the men had been hospitalized
at least once and reported a total of 329 hospitalizations.

CRIMINAL RECIDIVISM—
THREE-YEAR FOLLOW-UP (39)

Detailed and systematic reports of subsequent arrests, convictions, and imprisonments of 218 of the original men were obtained

45

through the Missouri Board of Probation and Parole. These were based upon Federal Bureau of Investigation records. At the end of his sentence, one man was transferred from the state prison to a federal prison to serve another sentence for a previous conviction in a federal court. He was not included in the follow-up analysis since he had not been exposed to the risk of recidivism. Systematic data were available for 217 of the original subjects. Concerning the other 5 men, only fragmentary information was available since FBI records were not provided to the Board of Probation and Parole. Therefore, these men were also excluded from the analysis. The follow-up data were obtained during the first three months of 1963, after an average follow-up of nearly three years.

Recidivism was measured in terms of percent rearrested at least once, mean number of rearrests, percent reimprisoned at least once, and mean number of reimprisonments. Nearly all reimprisonments were for felonies. Recidivism rates as functions of criminal status, type of crime, race, and age are summarized in Table 3.

The flat-timers had higher values for each measure of recidivism than the parolees. Although murderers had less difficulty than other criminals, the small number of cases prevented the differences from being significant. Check forgery was the only category of crime that differed significantly from the others with regard to percent reimprisoned and mean number of reimprisonments. Check forgers were also rearrested more frequently, but the differences were not significant. Half of the check offenders' reimprisonments were for new check crimes.

Blacks had a higher mean number of rearrests than whites. Compared to younger men, a lower percentage of men 40 and older were rearrested, and they experienced a smaller number of arrests. While the older men had fewer reimprisonments as well, the differences were not significant. Differences with educational achievement were inconsistent, and only one significant difference was found. A smaller percentage of men with 9 to 11 years of schooling were reimprisoned compared to all the others.

No significant differences were found in any of the recidivism measures with regard to family history of prison, history of pa-

TABLE 3
RECIDIVISM: MALE FELONS: 3-YEAR FOLLOW-UP (39)

Sample	N	Rearrested		Reimprisoned	
		%	Mean	%	Mean
Total sample	217	68	1.64	41	.53
Parolees[a]	116	57	1.28	28	.35
Flat-timers	101	81	2.04	56	.73
Burglary	89	75	1.96	47	.61
Larceny	46	70	1.72	50	.65
Robbery	32	66	1.78	34	.38
Car theft	18	72	1.67	50	.61
Check forgery[b]	18	89	2.39	78	1.06
Murder	12	42	1.17	17	.17
Rape	11	73	.91	44	.44
Whites[c]	160	66	1.41	43	.55
Blacks	57	74	2.40	35	.46
< Age 20[d]	58	71	1.48	41	.57
20-29	93	74	1.92	44	.58
30-39	37	59	1.97	41	.49
40-	29	38	.62	31	.31

[a] Each of the differences between the parolees and "flat-timers" is significant at the .01 level.
[b] The check offenders are significantly higher at the .01 level in percent imprisoned and mean number of imprisonments when compared to the entire group.
[c] The difference between whites and blacks for mean number of arrests is significant at the .05 level.
[d] The differences between those age 40 and over and all the others for percent arrested and mean number of arrests is significant at the .01 level.

(From J. Nerv. Ment. Dis. *138:* 575-580, 1964, copyright Williams and Wilkins. Reprinted by permission.)

rental divorce or separation, history of parental desertion, or history of having been raised by friends, relatives, or in institutions.

Recidivism as a function of psychiatric diagnosis is summarized in Table 4. Values for each diagnosis with 10 or more cases are presented. The total sample was too small for statistical analyses in which parolee–flat-timer status, age, and diagnosis were controlled for separately. Sociopathy, alcoholism, and drug depend-

TABLE 4

RECIDIVISM AND PSYCHIATRIC DIAGNOSIS: MALE FELONS:
3-YEAR FOLLOW-UP* (39)

| | N | Rearrested | | Reimprisoned | |
		%	Mean	%	Mean
Sociopathy	174	72	1.81	41	.53
Alcoholism	96	74	1.97	45	.59
Drug Dependence	10	90	2.10	50	.70
Anxiety Neurosis	26	62	1.73	35	.46

* Differences between sociopaths and nonsociopaths and between alcoholics
and nonalcoholics in percent and mean number of rearrests significant at the
.05 level.

(From J. Nerv. Ment. Dis. 138: 575-580, 1964, copyright Williams and
Wilkins. Reprinted by permission.)

ence were associated with higher recidivism rates though only
some of the differences were significant.

The high recidivism rates for the entire sample, and particularly for flat-timers, indicate the generally unfavorable prognosis
for convicted criminals. This is all the more striking in view of
the brief follow-up, less than three years. In general, the main
difference we observed between parolees and flat-timers at the
beginning of the study was in the extent of their previous criminal career: 27 percent of the parolees had been in prison prior to
the index crime compared to 80 percent of the flat-timers. Furthermore, 67 percent of the flat-timers had previously been paroled compared to only 12 percent of the parolees. The parolees
had been paroled following the index crimes because they had
had less trouble and had been regarded as better risks. The findings at follow-up support the judgment of the parole board. The
very high rearrest rate (81 percent) and reimprisonment rate (56
percent) of the flat-timers may have obscured the importance of
other factors by submerging other possible differences. The results indicate, however, that the single most important variable in
predicting recidivism among convicted criminals is the extent of
their prior criminal career.

Recidivism rates associated with check forgery are of interest.

Check offenders differed from other criminals in race (they were all white), age (they were older), educational achievement (greater than other criminals), and an increased prevalence of alcoholism. The increased reimprisonment rates are particularly striking since there were no significant positive associations between reimprisonment and race, age, education, or alcoholism. There appears to be something specific about check forgery that makes for significantly higher recidivism rates. The high reimprisonment rate for new check offenses is consistent.

A higher mean number of rearrests for blacks was the only significant racial difference in recidivism. This probably represents primarily an increased risk of being arrested for "suspicion" or "investigation" on the part of former black felons. The significantly ($p < .01$) lower reconviction rate for blacks (20 percent) compared to whites (39 percent) suggests that this is the correct explanation. The conviction rate is the number of convictions and imprisonments divided by the number of arrests, or the ratio of the mean number of imprisonments divided by the mean number of arrests.

The significantly lower rearrest rates and lower reimprisonment rates for men 40 and older indicate that criminal recidivism falls as middle age is approached or reached. Various speculative interpretations have been proposed to account for this observation: maturation, falling-off of aggressive drives, and the like.

The absence of any effect of family history and parental home variables upon recidivism is noteworthy, since it might have been expected that individuals from the poorer family backgrounds would have experienced higher recidivism rates. It would appear that such variables, while associated with an increased risk of becoming a criminal, do not influence the subsequent criminal career once a man has been convicted of a criminal act.

Aside from sociopathy, alcoholism, and drug dependence, anxiety neurosis was the only psychiatric disorder encountered with any but minimal frequency. Anxiety neurosis was not associated with recidivism rates different from the total sample. As already noted, considerable overlap occurred in the diagnoses of sociopathy, alcoholism, and drug dependence. Since many of the arrests of the alcoholics were for "drunkenness" and other misdemeanors probably associated with intoxication (such as fighting and traffic offenses), the increased arrest history associated with the three disorders may only reflect the increased frequency with which alcoholics were arrested for behavior directly related to being intoxicated. In other words, alcoholics may not have shown an increased recidivism rate aside from these kinds of misdemeanors. Because routine police records are not always clear about the reasons for many arrests, no final conclusions are possible. The more important measure of recidivism—the rate of reimprisonment—was not significantly greater for individuals with any of these disorders compared to the rest of the sample.

To summarize: after three years of follow-up, relative youth and extent of prior criminal career were associated with significantly increased risks of recidivism. Psychiatric diagnoses seemed to play only a limited role *once a man had been convicted of a felony.*

CRIMINAL RECIDIVISM, ALCOHOLISM, AND PAROLE EXPERIENCES (43)

The original sample included 121 parolees. As already noted, each of the criminal recidivism measures was higher for alcoholic than nonalcoholic subjects, but only the arrest differences were statistically significant. In order to examine further the possible association between alcoholism and recidivism, the parole office records of the parolees were studied.

Of the original 121 parolees, 48 were alcoholics, 15 were questionable alcoholics, and 58 were nonalcoholics. The detailed, systematic reports of subsequent arrests, convictions, and prison experiences described above were available for 116 of the 121 parolees: 48 alcoholics, 13 questionable alcoholics, and 55 nonalcoholics. During the summer of 1963, the parole office record for each of the 121 parolees was abstracted systematically. At the time, 12 men, or 10 percent, were still being followed under parole. The others had been discharged from parole because it had been completed or revoked. The average period of supervision to the time of the study was just under three years, with a range of from one to 53 months. All comments concerning drinking were noted and recorded. The findings described below refer to the 116 parolees for whom recidivism rates were available.

Parole record comments concerning drinking are summarized in Tables 5, 6, and 7. Table 5 indicates that nearly half of all records included some reference to heavy drinking. The frequency of such notations varied from 71 percent for the records of alcoholics to 20 percent for the records of nonalcoholics, with an intermediate figure of 54 percent for questionable alcoholics. The differences between alcoholics and nonalcoholics and between questionable alcoholics and nonalcoholics were statistically significant. These differences indicated that the original diagnostic criteria for alcoholism were valid because the frequency of notations about excessive drinking paralleled the certainty of the diagnosis of alcoholism, and the observations leading to the notations were made without any knowledge of the alcoholism diagnoses.

Tables 6 and 7 present, for questionable alcoholics and nonalcoholics respectively, the kinds of comments abstracted. They re-

TABLE 5

PAROLE RECORD INDICATIONS OF HEAVY DRINKING: MALE FELONS (43)

Original Diagnosis	N	Parole Record Indication of Heavy Drinking %*
Alcoholics	48	71
Questionable alcoholics	13	54
Nonalcoholics	55	20
Total	116	45

* Difference between alcoholics and nonalcoholics significant at the .01 level. Difference between questionable alcoholics and nonalcoholics significant at the .05 level.
Difference between alcoholics and questionable alcoholics not significant.

(From Am. J. Psychiatry 122: 436-439, 1965, copyright 1965 by The American Psychiatric Association. Reprinted by permission.)

TABLE 6

ORIGINAL QUESTIONABLE ALCOHOLICS WITH HEAVY
DRINKING NOTATIONS IN PAROLE RECORDS: MALE
FELONS (43)

Comments
Probably was drunk on night he was picked up the final time before parole was revoked.
Intoxicated at time of arrest and admitted to several episodes of excessive drinking at this time.
Reported frequently in bars. Arrested in bar for fighting and disturbing the peace.
Drinking binge after wife left him.
Repeated excessive drinking leading to fights. Attacked companions on two separate occasions with knives while drinking heavily.
Reported to be drinking excessively by officials at "half-way house" for criminals.
Recurrent heavy drinking according to relative. Heavy drinking before new crime.

(From Am. J. Psychiatry *122:* 436-439, 1965, copyright 1965 by The American Psychiatric Association. Reprinted by permission.)

veal the serious nature of the drinking and emphasize the frequent personal and social complications.

The category of questionable alcoholism deserves further comment. These men were omitted originally when comparisons were made between alcoholics and nonalcoholics because their alcoholic status was not certain. With the additional information available from the parole records, it seemed appropriate to review the alcoholism diagnoses. The additional information did not warrant any change in diagnosis for those previously considered to be definite alcoholics; nothing was found that cast doubt upon the original diagnosis. For 7 of the original questionable alcoholics, additional data indicated continued problems associated with drinking, but none of these diagnoses was changed because the specific criteria for the diagnosis of alcoholism were still not met. Problems associated with drinking were recorded for 11 of

TABLE 7
ORIGINAL NONALCOHOLICS WITH HEAVY DRINKING
NOTATIONS IN PAROLE RECORD: MALE FELONS (43)

Comments
Arrested for driving while intoxicated and for driving without a license.
Relatives called on separate occasions and complained of heavy drinking and abuse of mother.
Arrested once for driving while intoxicated and once for trying to buy liquor while under age.
"Half-way house" reported that he was drunk, disorderly, and has absconded.
Arrested for driving in stolen auto and for driving while drinking. Also was drinking at time of new offense.
"Half-way house" reported excessive drinking on several occasions. Missing work because of drinking. Found drunk at home by parole officer. Joined AA. Fired because of drinking. "Blackouts" reported.
Parole officer warned subject about his heavy drinking.
Fired because of drinking. Drinking and threatening neighbor with a gun.
Arrested for drunkenness. Wife reported him for heavy drinking and absconding.
Fired for drinking and refusing to go to work. Beat up girl while drinking.
Heavy drinking reported prior to absconding.
Mother and brother reported repeated heavy drinking at taverns. Arrested for drinking.

(From Am. J. Psychiatry 122: 436-439, 1965, copyright 1965 by The American Psychiatric Association. Reprinted by permission.)

the 55 original nonalcoholics. For 2 of these, a diagnosis of alcoholism was now appropriate based on all the available information; the other 9 were rediagnosed as questionable alcoholics.

Recidivism rates for these revised categories of alcoholism as well as rates for the entire parolee sample for comparison are presented in Table 8. Alcoholics showed significantly higher rates than nonalcoholics for percent rearrested, mean number of rearrests, and percent reimprisoned. Questionable alcoholics showed

TABLE 8

RECIDIVISM RATE RELATED TO REVISED ALCOHOLISM
DIAGNOSES: MALE FELONS (43)

Revised Alcoholism Diagnosis	N	Rearrested		Reimprisoned	
		%	Mean	%	Mean
Alcoholics[a]	50	62	1.62	30	.38
Questionable alcoholics[b]	22	86	1.68	55	.64
Total heavy drinkers[c]	72	69	1.64	38	.46
Nonalcoholics	44	39	.75	11	.16
Total parolees	116	57	1.28	28	.35

[a] The differences between the alcoholics and nonalcoholics in percent rearrested, mean rearrests, and percent reimprisoned are significant at the .05 level. The differences between alcoholics and questionable alcoholics in percent reimprisoned and mean reimprisonments are significant at the .05 level.
[b] The differences between the questionable alcoholics and nonalcoholics in percent rearrested, percent reimprisoned, and mean reimprisonments are significant at the .01 level while the difference for mean rearrests is significant at the .05 level.
[c] The differences between the total heavy drinkers and the nonalcoholics in percent rearrested and percent reimprisoned were significant at the .01 level while the differences for mean rearrests and mean reimprisonments were significant at the .05 level.

(From Am. J. Psychiatry *122:* 436-439, 1965, copyright 1965 by The American Psychiatric Association. Reprinted by permission.)

significantly higher rates than nonalcoholics for all four measures. Total problem drinkers (alcoholics plus questionable alcoholics) showed significantly higher rates than nonalcoholics for all four measures. And questionable alcoholics showed significantly higher rates than alcoholics for percent reimprisoned and mean number of reimprisonments.

To summarize: alcoholism appeared to be associated with an increased risk of criminal recidivism. The additional data from the parole records, showing that the original alcoholism diagnoses of the parolees needed revision, imply that similar changes might be appropriate for some of the flat-timers, if analogous records were available. This, in turn, might have led to an increased reimprisonment rate for all alcoholic felons (flat-timers as well as parolees) that would have achieved statistical significance.

PSYCHIATRIC DISORDERS IN
FIRST-DEGREE RELATIVES (51, 52)

Psychiatric diagnoses for interviewed relatives are presented in Tables 9 and 10. Psychiatric hospitalization and suicide attempts are presented in Table 11. Most of the interviewed relatives were free of psychiatric illness; this was true for each sex-race group except for black men, only 40 percent of whom were free of psychiatric illness. Most black men with psychiatric diagnosis, however, were sociopaths or alcoholics.

Turning to individual psychiatric disorders, no interviewed relative received a diagnosis of obsessional neurosis, dementia, or schizophrenia. No discussion is required about the absence of obsessional neurosis or dementia since these disorders are generally not thought to be associated with criminality, but the absence of schizophrenia requires comment because such an association is suspected by many. Schizophrenia was recognized in only one percent of the index subjects, a prevalence similar to that in the

TABLE 9
OVERALL PSYCHIATRIC DIAGNOSES: INTERVIEWED RELATIVES
OF MALE FELONS (51)

	White Men (N=71) %	Black Men (N=31) %	Total Men (N=102) %	White Women (N=112) %	Black Women (N=46) %	Total Women (N=158) %	Total (N=260) %
No Psychiatric Disorder*	60	40	54	52	72	58	56
Some Psychiatric Disorder*	40	60	46	48	28	42	44

There were three families with two index subjects each in the original sample. In the first family, the two index cases were brothers; their father, who was an alcoholic, was counted twice. In the second family, the two index cases were father and son; the daughter (or sister) was free of psychiatric illness and she was counted twice. In the third family, the two index cases were brothers; their mother and half-brother, both free of psychiatric illness, were each counted twice. (The first and third families were white; the second family was black.)

From Dis. Nerv. Syst. 28: 651-659, 1967. Reprinted by permission.)

TABLE 10

INDIVIDUAL PSYCHIATRIC DIAGNOSES: INTERVIEWED RELATIVES
OF MALE FELONS (51)

	White Men (N=71) %	Black Men (N=31) %	Total Men (N=102) %	White Women (N=112) %	Black Women (N=46) %	Total Women (N=158) %	Total (N=260) %
Obsessional Neurosis	0	0	0	0	0	0	0
Anxiety Neurosis	7	0	5	9	13	10	8
Brain Syndrome	0	0	0	0	0	0	0
Schizophrenia	0	0	0	0	0	0	0
Primary Affective Disorder	1	0	1	2	0	1	1
Homosexuality	3	0	2	0	0	0	1
Briquet's Syndrome (Hysteria)	0	0	0	4	5	4	3
Probable Briquet's Syndrome (Hysteria)	0	0	0	2	0	1	1
Total Briquet's Syndrome (Hysteria)	0	0	0	6	5	5	4
Sociopathy	13	23	16	3	0	2	7
Questionable Sociopathy	1	6	3	2	0	1	2
Total Sociopathy	14	29	19	5	0	3	9
Alcoholism	13	23	16	2	2	2	7
Questionable Alcoholism	14	26	18	2	4	3	8
Total Alcoholism	27	49	34	4	6	5	15
Drug Dependence	1	3	2	0	0	0	1
Questionable Drug Dependence	1	3	2	0	0	0	1
Total Drug Dependence	2	6	4	0	0	0	2
Undiagnosed	7	9	8	30	10	25	18

(From Dis. Nerv. Syst. 28: 651-659, 1967. Reprinted by permission.)

TABLE 11

OTHER CLINICAL DATA: INTERVIEWED RELATIVES
OF MALE FELONS (51)

	White Men (N=71) %	Black Men (N=31) %	Total Men (N=102) %	White Women (N=112) %	Black Women (N=46) %	Total Women (N=158) %	Total (N=260) %
History of Psychiatric Hospitalization*	0	6	2	4	0	3	2
History of Attempted Suicide†	1	0	1	2	0	1	1

* The diagnoses in these subjects were: hysteria (a white woman), alcoholism plus questionable drug dependence (a black man), sociopathy (a black man), undiagnosed: questionable primary affective disorder (two white women), and undiagnosed: cancer plus secondary depression (a white woman).
† The diagnoses in these subjects were: alcoholism plus questionable drug dependence (a white man) and undiagnosed: questionable primary affective disorder (two white women).

(From Dis. Nerv. Syst. 28: 651-659, 1967. Reprinted by permission.)

general population. It might have been suspected that other cases of schizophrenia were either not recognized or were diagnosed as some other condition. If this had been true, an increased prevalence of schizophrenia would have been anticipated in the first-degree relatives of index subjects, since schizophrenia has been repeatedly found to be more common in families of index cases than the general population. The failure to find an increased prevalence of schizophrenia among interviewed relatives indicates that this disorder was not missed or incorrectly diagnosed in the index subjects.

Anxiety neurosis was recognized in 8 percent of the interviewed relatives; it was about twice as frequent among women as men. The 8 percent in this study, like the 12 percent in the index subjects, is probably not very far from the general population prevalence.

The prevalence of primary affective disorder among the interviewed relatives was only one percent; women were more often affected than men. Because of great variability in diagnostic terms and criteria, estimated population rates for this condition vary, but general psychiatric experience suggests that primary affective disorders probably occur at rates somewhat higher than that found here. The absence of reliable population rates is particularly important in evaluating undiagnosed cases reporting a mild, questionably significant depression in the past. This was reported by 7 percent of the interviewed relatives. These individuals reported no disability from or medical attention for these depressions; thus, only a careful population study could determine whether or not the experience of these relatives differed from that of the general population.

Homosexuality was found in only 2 percent of the male relatives and in none of the female relatives. These frequencies are lower than those estimated for the general population by Kinsey (62, 63).

Since hysteria (Briquet's Syndrome) as defined in this study is seen primarily in women, its prevalence among female relatives is the important figure. Hysteria or probable hysteria was found in 5 percent of the interviewed female relatives. In addition, among the undiagnosed group of women, another two percent were suffering from a disorder suggesting hysteria that failed to meet the specific criteria. Thus, Briquet's Syndrome was found about three times more commonly among the female relatives than in the general female population, where the prevalence is between one and 2 percent (103). Yet it was not quite as frequent as in first-degree female relatives of patients with hysteria where it occurs in about 19 percent (1, 101). The family study of hysteria cited (1) also revealed an increased prevalence of sociopathy and alcoholism in first-degree male relatives of index cases. It thus anticipated the present findings of an apparently increased prevalence of hysteria among first-degree female relatives of men convicted of serious crimes, who were also frequently alcoholics, and of whom nearly 80 percent were sociopaths. This will be discussed further below.

Sociopathy and questionable sociopathy were diagnosed among

the male relatives in 16 percent and 3 percent respectively and among female relatives in 2 percent and one percent respectively. Population figures using the same criteria are not available, but the high prevalence rates for this disorder, particularly among male relatives, strongly suggest that its incidence increases among relatives of male felons. Further, 65 percent of the interviewed first-degree relatives who had ever been jailed and 100 percent of those who had ever been convicted of a felony were sociopaths.

Alcoholism was diagnosed in 16 percent of the men and 2 percent of the women; questionable alcoholism in 18 percent of the men and 3 percent of the women. Thus, over a third of the men and 5 percent of the women reported difficulties associated with heavy drinking. While population figures for alcoholism using these diagnostic criteria are not available, studies using similar criteria indicate population prevalence rates considerably below those of this study (103). The findings indicate, therefore, an increased prevalence of alcoholism among the relatives.

Drug dependence and questionable drug dependence were seen only among interviewed male relatives. The total prevalence among the male relatives was 4 percent. All of these men were also alcoholics. This rate, similar to that of the index subjects, suggests an increased prevalence of drug dependence among male relatives, but the absence of accurate population rates for comparison limits the confidence to be placed in the conclusion.

An undiagnosed group of 18 percent (8 percent of men and 25 percent of women) is not surprising in a study using explicit criteria. It should be emphasized that there were no cases of possible schizophrenia in this group, and that nearly all of the undiagnosed subjects appeared to be suffering from illnesses similar to anxiety neurosis or hysteria or had experienced very mild depressions in the past.

Diagnoses and other clinical data concerning noninterviewed relatives are summarized in Table 12. These findings from the family histories are similar to those from the personal interviews. In particular, they confirm the high prevalence of alcoholism and sociopathy among first-degree relatives of convicted criminals. It has been shown that 28 percent of the original alcoholism diag-

TABLE 12

FAMILY HISTORY DATA ABOUT NONINTERVIEWED RELATIVES
OF MALE FELONS (51)*

	White Men (N=108) %	Black Men (N=50) %	Total Men (N=158) %	White Women (N=73) %	Black Women (N=28) %	Total Women (N=101) %	Total (N=259 %
Brain Syndrome							
Suspected	0	0	0	1	0	1	<1
Schizophrenia							
Suspected	0	0	0	1	0	1	<1
Primary Affective Disorder							
Suspected	2	0	1	1	0	1	1
Sociopathy							
Suspected	19	26	21	0	0	0	13
Alcoholism							
Suspected	21	10	18	1	7	3	12
History of Psychiatric Hospitalization†	<1	0	<1	4	0	3	<2
History of Attempted Suicide‡	<1	0	<1	1	0	1	<1
History of Completed Suicide	0	0	0	0	0	0	0

* See footnote to Table 9 for remarks about those families represented twice among the index cases. A mother of the index cases in the first family, who was reported to be without psychiatric difficulties, was counted twice. A male relative in the second family was the brother of one index case and the son of the other index case; he was counted twice and was reported as a questionable sociopath because of recurrent delinquency and police troubles. The father, a sister, and a brother of the index cases in the third family were each counted twice and were reported to be free of psychiatric difficulties.

† The diagnoses in these subjects were: questionable primary affective disorder (a white man and a white woman), questionable schizophrenia (a white woman), and questionable brain syndrome (a white woman).

‡ The diagnoses in these subjects were: questionable primary affective disorder (a white man and a white woman).

(From Dis. Nerv. Syst. 28: 651-659, 1967. Reprinted by permission.)

noses in the felons would not have been suspected from what relatives reported about the felons (50). If the same percentage applies here, the corrected figures for alcoholism in Table 12 would be 25 percent for men and 5 percent for women—similar to those for interviewed relatives.

To summarize: most of the first-degree relatives of convicted felons were free of psychiatric illness, and the only psychiatric disorders seen more frequently among such relatives than among the general population were sociopathy, alcoholism, drug dependence, and hysteria. The first 3 were encountered chiefly among male relatives and hysteria was found only among female relatives. In addition, the first 3 disorders, whether among index subjects or among relatives, were frequently seen in the same individual. Table 13 demonstrates the association among these 3 diagnoses. It deals only with male relatives because the index subjects were male, and the 3 disorders were seen chiefly among male relatives.

A principal reason for studying first-degree relatives was to evaluate the validity of the psychiatric diagnoses made in the index study of convicted felons. A family study was necessary to be sure that there were no unrecognized psychiatric disorders among the index subjects. If there had been such unrecognized disorders among the index subjects, it would have been reasonable to expect an increased frequency among the first-degree relatives, since an increased familial aggregation has been demonstrated for all of the common psychiatric disorders. To put it another way, first-degree relatives of subjects with a specific psychiatric illness would be expected to present prevalence rates for the same illness significantly higher than those found in the general population and, at the same time, rates for unrelated psychiatric illnesses similar to those found in the general population. Further, if first-degree relatives showed increased prevalence rates for a different psychiatric disorder, it would suggest a significant relationship between the two illnesses. The exact nature of the relationship would require further study to determine whether the 2 illnesses were simply interchangeable clinical forms of the same basic condition, whether the two illnesses were both caused by the same

TABLE 13

ASSOCIATION AMONG DIAGNOSES OF SOCIOPATHY, ALCOHOLISM, AND DRUG DEPENDENCE*# (51)

	Index Subjects (Male) (N=223)		Interviewed Male Relatives (N=102)		Noninterviewed Male Relatives (N=158)	
	Sociopathy (N=176) %	Others (N=47) %	Sociopathy (N=19) %	Others (N=83) %	Sociopathy (N=33) %	Others (N=125) %
Alcoholism	61 #	32	73 #	24	48 #	10
Drug Dependence	6 #	0	21 #	0	Not Known	Not Known
Alcoholism or Drug Dependence	64 #	32	73 #	24	Not Known	Not Known
	Alcoholism (N=121) %	Others (N=102) %	Alcoholism (N=34) %	Others (N=68) %	Alcoholism (N=28) %	Others (N=130) %
Sociopathy	88 #	70	38 #	9	57 #	13
Drug Dependence	3	6	12 #	0	Not Known	Not Known
Sociopathy or Drug Dependence	88 #	70	38 #	9	Not Known	Not Known
	Drug Depend. (N=10) %	Others (N=213) %	Drug Depend. (N=4) %	Others (N=98) %	Drug Depend. (N=?) %	Others (N=?) %
Sociopathy	100	78	100 #	0	Not Known	Not Known
Alcoholism	40	55	100 #	0	Not Known	Not Known
Sociopathy or Alcoholism	100	85	100 #	0	Not Known	Not Known

* Each diagnostic group includes those subjects with questionable as well as definite diagnoses.

This symbol between values indicates that the difference is significant at better than the .01 level (the difference is more than 2.5 times the S.E. of the difference).

(From Dis. Nerv. Syst. *28:* 651-659, 1967. Reprinted by permission.)

etiologic factors, or whether one illness predisposed the population to the other illness.

The family study thus supported the validity of the original diagnoses since increased prevalence rates of the same illnesses were found among first-degree relatives.

On the basis of the work reported thus far, the following conclusions were reached concerning the association between criminality and psychiatric illness. The great majority of convicted male felons are sociopaths. This is another way of saying that they have a history of recurrent delinquency, antisocial behavior, and poor adjustment in school, job, and marriage, that begins in childhood or adolescence and continues into adulthood. Many such criminals are alcoholics or drug dependent, with rates for these disorders higher among those with sociopathy than among the others. There is an increased rate of criminality among first-degree relatives of felons, and most of these criminal relatives are also sociopaths. There are increased rates of alcoholism and drug dependence among relatives largely associated with sociopathy. Finally, there appears to be an increased prevalence of hysteria among female relatives.

EIGHT-TO-NINE-YEAR FOLLOW-UP:
PSYCHIATRIC DIAGNOSES (46)

The follow-up interviews were conducted between July 1967 and October 1968. The interviewers, though familiar with the results of the study up to that point, did not know the individual diagnoses of the men, nor did they consult the original interview until after the follow-up interview. The follow-up interviews were conducted in hospitals, private homes, jails, places of work, airports, hotel rooms, and, in a small number of cases, via long distance telephone. Men were found and interviewed in nearly half of all states, from New Hampshire to California and from Florida to Washington. Each individual received, in addition to any travel expenses, ten dollars if he came to a place convenient to the interviewer or five dollars if the interview was conducted at the subject's home. Because of unusual circumstances, a few subjects received twenty dollars.

Research assistants kept a detailed log of the search for each individual, including all contacts with the subject, his friends, relatives, employers, and police. All kinds of records were gathered: police, prison, parole, hospital, clinic, private physician, vital statistics, military service, insurance, and so forth. Of the original 223 men, 209, or 94 percent, were located. The other 14, or 6 percent, could not be found. Among the 209 located men were 5 who had died, 2 who were abroad, 26 who refused to be interviewed or who were so uncooperative that they were considered refusals, and 176 who were interviewed personally.

The dead men had died an average of three years after the initial interview. Their average age at death was 48, ranging from 21 to 81. Two were black. Two were married and one was a widower, having murdered his wife (the index crime). At the original interview, sociopathy and alcoholism were diagnosed in each of the 5 men. Two were definite alcoholics and 3 were questionable. No other diagnoses had been made. At least 2 of the men had been involved in another felony subsequent to the original study. The causes of death, obtained from their death certificates, were: cancer of the liver with cirrhosis, bullet wound of the heart, bronchial pneumonia, auto accident, and a stab wound of the heart. Thus, 3 died a violent death, and a fourth probably from liver complications of alcoholism.

One of the 2 men who were abroad was with the army in Vietnam; the other had been deported to Frankfurt, Germany. The 176 interviewed men represented 79 percent of the original sample and 87 percent of those located alive in the United States.

Table 14 presents the diagnoses made at the time of the first interview for the 176 men interviewed at follow-up as well as the diagnoses made originally for the entire sample of 223 men. The men interviewed at follow-up did not differ from the full sample in the distribution of psychiatric diagnoses. Further, none of the men who refused interview was in a psychiatric hospital or, so far as could be determined, was receiving psychiatric treatment at the time of contact. Similar proportions of parolees and flat-

TABLE 14

PSYCHIATRIC DIAGNOSES AT 8-9-YEAR FOLLOW-UP:
MALE FELONS (46)

Diagnosis	Diagnosis At Original Interview	Diagnosis At Original Interview	Diagnosis At Follow-up Interview	Diagnosis At Both Interviews	Diagnosis At Either Interview
	Full Sample N = 223	← Men Seen At Follow-up → N = 176			
	%	%	%	%	%
Anxiety Neurosis	12	12	9	2	17
Briquet's Syndrome (Hysteria)	0	0	0	0	0
Obsessional Neurosis	0	0	0	0	0
Schizophrenia	1	1	1	<1	2
Primary Affective Disorder	0	0	0	0	0
Brain Syndrome	<1	0	2	0	2
Sociopathy					
Definite	79	78	56	52	81
Questionable	0	0	4	0	4
Total	79	78	60		
Either				56	81
Alcoholism					
Definite	43	43	39	26	56
Questionable	11	12	15	<1	26
Total	54	55	54		
Either				40	67
Drug Dependence					
Definite	5	7	9	5	11
Questionable	0	0	4	0	4
Total	5	7	13		
Either				6	14
Homosexuality					
Ever	8	10	14	6	18
Significant	<1	<1	0	0	<1
Undiagnosed	<1	0	5	0	5

(Slightly modified from Arch. Gen. Psychiatry 20: 583-591, 1969, copyright 1969 by the American Medical Association. Reprinted by permission.)

timers were interviewed: 77 percent of the former and 81 percent of the latter. Seventy-seven percent of the white men were interviewed compared to 85 percent of the black men. None of the differences between interviewed subjects and the total sample is statistically significant, indicating that psychiatric illness, criminal classification, and race did not determine which of the men it was possible to interview at follow-up.

Table 14 also presents the percentages of diagnoses made at follow-up, at both interviews, and at either interview, for the 176 men followed and interviewed. There was some inconsistency of diagnosis between the two interviews, but the distribution of diagnoses at follow-up was similar to that seen at the initial study. Again, the principal psychiatric disorders were sociopathy, alcoholism, and drug dependence. The results of the two interviews indicate that sociopathy was present in from 56 to 81 percent of the men, alcoholism in from 40 to 67 percent, and drug dependence in from 6 to 14 percent.

Anxiety neurosis was seen in from 2 to 17 percent, but no cases of obsessional neurosis or hysteria were found.

Three men received the diagnosis of schizophrenia at least once. The 2 men who received this diagnosis originally were both studied at follow-up. One man received the diagnosis at each interview, another only at the first, and the third man only at follow-up. On the basis of all information available at follow-up, the second man probably suffered from a schizophreniform reaction associated with the illicit use of drugs that cleared completely before follow-up. The third man was somewhat paranoid at the time of the first interview, but this was not considered significant. By the time of follow-up, however, it was apparent that the original paranoid ideas were the beginning of a chronic delusional disorder.

No man received the diagnosis of primary affective disorder at either point in the study. At follow-up, 3 men reported at least one episode of significant depression. These were considered secondary depressions (53) since each man received the diagnosis of sociopathy and alcoholism at both interviews; one of these men also received the diagnoses of anxiety neurosis and brain syndrome at follow-up.

One man with brain syndrome at the original interview was not followed. Three other men received the diagnosis of brain syndrome at follow-up. One was described in the previous paragraph. The second also received the diagnosis of sociopathy and epilepsy at both interviews. The third was considered to be a sociopath at both interviews and a questionable alcoholic at follow-up.

The percentage of men reporting any homosexual experience was between 6 and 18, but the only man who was originally considered significantly homosexual denied any homosexuality at follow-up.

There was one subject with an undiagnosed disorder in the original study. He was not among the men seen at follow-up. Eight men received this diagnosis at follow-up, though for 5 it was in addition to definite diagnoses of both sociopathy and alcoholism. Four of the 8 reported a chronic anxiety neurosislike disorder without cardiorespiratory symptoms. Two other men reported depressions that did not meet the diagnostic criteria; they required medical attention, though only one saw a psychiatrist. This man (with diagnoses of sociopathy and alcoholism at both interviews) had received electric convulsive therapy as a psychiatric in-patient. The seventh man complained only of mild palpitation but had been in group psychotherapy for several years. The last man was in a psychiatric hospital with symptoms suggesting schizophrenia. He was considered undiagnosed because of a history of excessive amphetamine use which made it impossible to rule out amphetamine psychosis.

DIAGNOSTIC CONSISTENCY (44, 45)

Four diagnoses were made frequently enough both originally and at follow-up to permit an assessment of the consistency of diagnosis: sociopathy, alcoholism, drug dependence, and anxiety neurosis. In addition, a history of any homosexual experience was also obtained often enough for such analysis. The patterns of each of these diagnoses are presented in Table 15.

Of those who originally received a diagnosis of sociopathy, 72 percent were so diagnosed (definite or questionable) at follow-up. Of those who did not receive this diagnosis originally, 18 percent received it at follow-up. For alcoholism (adding definite and questionable cases) the corresponding figures were 74 percent and 28 percent; for drug dependence, 90 percent and 8 percent; for anxiety neurosis, 29 percent and 6 percent; and for any homosexuality 59 percent and 9 percent.

Since the index and follow-up studies involved similar interviews conducted by different interviewers eight to nine years apart, it was possible to analyze further the consistency of the history and the stability of diagnosis with regard to at least two diagnoses: sociopathy and alcoholism. These diagnoses were made frequently enough to permit a quantitative evaluation of consistency.

TABLE 15

PATTERNS OF DIAGNOSES AMONG THE 176 MALE FELONS
STUDIED AT 8-9-YEAR FOLLOW-UP (46)

Diagnosis At Original Interview	Diagnosis At Follow-up Interview	Socio-pathy %	Alcohol-ism %	Drug Depend-ence %	Anxiety Neurosis %	Homo-sexuality Ever %
Definite	Definite	52	26	5	3	6
Definite	Questionable	4	7	1	<1	
Definite	None	22	10	<1	8	4
Questionable	Definite		7			
Questionable	Questionable		<1			
Questionable	None		4			
None	Definite	3	6	5	5	8
None	Questionable	<1	7	3		
None	None	19	33	86	83	82

Consistency of Drinking History and Diagnosis of Alcoholism

As part of the two interviews, a systematic drinking history was elicited based on 17 questions (see Table 17), the answers to which served as the basis for the diagnosis of alcoholism. At both interviews each question was phrased so as to learn whether the drinking manifestation had ever occurred; thus a lifetime history was sought—not just the drinking picture at a particular time. Remission of alcoholism was not of concern here.

Table 16 presents the pattern of alcoholism diagnoses in the two interviews. Nearly three-quarters of the men who received an alcoholism diagnosis (definite or questionable) in the first interview received one of these diagnoses at follow-up. Definite and questionable alcoholism differed only in the number and range of symptoms; in either case, excessive drinking associated with personal, social, or medical complications was present. Twenty-six percent of the definite alcoholics in the first interview were considered to be nonalcoholics at follow-up; symptoms considered positive at the first interview were denied or minimized at follow-up. The 43 men who received the diagnosis of definite alcoholism at both interviews (the "consistent" group) and the 19 men considered nonalcoholic at the second interview after having

TABLE 16
PATTERN OF ALCOHOLISM DIAGNOSIS IN THE TWO
INTERVIEWS: MALE FELONS (45)

1st Interview		2nd Interview			
Diagnosis	N	Definite Alcoholic	Questionable Alcoholic	Total Alcoholic	Not Alcoholic
Definite Alcoholic	73	43 (59%)	11 (15%)	54 (74%)	19 (26%)
Questionable Alcoholic	18	12 (67%)	0 (0%)	12 (67%)	6 (33%)
Total Alcoholic	91	55 (60%)	11 (12%)	66 (73%)	25 (27%)
Not Alcoholic	85	14 (16%)	13 (15%)	27 (32%)	58 (68%)
TOTAL	176	69 (39%)	24 (14%)	93 (53%)	83 (47%)

(From Q. J. Stud. Alcohol *33*: 111-116, 1972, copyright 1972 by J. Stud. Alcohol, Inc., New Brunswick, N.J. 08903. Reprinted by permission.)

received the diagnosis of definite alcoholism at the first (the "inconsistent" group) were compared on a wide range of demographic, clinical, and social variables. The inconsistent subjects were more likely to be black (42 percent versus 12 percent, p < .01). They also reported fewer alcoholism symptoms at the first interview (mean number of symptoms: 4.8 versus 8.4, p < .001; 7 or more symptoms: 16 percent versus 70 percent, p < .001). The two groups did not differ with regard to sociopathy, drug dependence, anxiety neurosis, or homosexuality at either interview, nor in the proportion whose history was positive for each of these other disorders at the first interview and negative at the second.

Table 17 presents the pattern of responses in the two interviews to the list of 17 questions. Table 18 presents for each question the number of "no" answers at follow-up by those who gave "yes" answers at the first interview. The findings are divided according to the total number of "yes" answers at the first interview. Inconsistency occurred with regard to each question. There were 604 "yes" answers at the first interview; of these, 44 percent became "no" at follow-up. The lowest average proportion of "no" answers at follow-up was given by those with 7 or more "yes" answers at the first interview; this was also true for nearly each alcoholism symptom individually. Among symptoms with the highest consistency were: "Has your family ever objected to your drinking?" "Did you ever think you drank too much in general?" "Have you ever been arrested for drinking or disturbing the peace?" "Have you ever been in fights when drinking?" Among those with the lowest consistency were: "Have you ever gone on benders?" "Have you ever wanted to stop drinking but couldn't?" "Did you ever drink things like hair tonic, rubbing alcohol, or other non-beverage alcohol?"

The data indicate the general limits to be expected in the consistency of the drinking history elicited during standardized interviews years apart. Whether similar results would be obtained from a noncriminal population must await other studies. But the findings warrant certain conclusions. If a diagnosis of definite or questionable alcoholism is made on the basis of a standardized

TABLE 17

PATTERN OF RESPONSES IN THE TWO INTERVIEWS TO
INDIVIDUAL ITEMS IN THE DRINKING HISTORY (45)
(N = 176)

	No Both Interv. %	Yes Both Interv. %	No 1st Interv. Yes 2nd Interv. %	Yes 1st Interv. No 2nd Interv. %
1. Has your family ever objected to your drinking?	36	35	9	20
2. Did you ever think you drank too much in general?	49	20	20	11
3. Have others, such as friends, physicians, clergymen, ever said you drank too much?	54	16	15	15
4. Have you ever felt guilty about drinking?	75	6	13	6
5. Have you ever lost friends because of drinking?	80	7	7	6
6. Did you ever get into trouble at work because of drinking?	78	6	11	5
7. Did you ever have trouble with driving because of drinking?	66	10	17	7
8. Have you ever been arrested for drinking or disturbing the peace?	52	23	14	11
9. Have you ever been in fights when drinking?	57	22	11	10
10. Have you ever wanted to stop drinking but couldn't?	85	1	9	5
11. Have you ever tried to control your drinking by trying to drink only under certain circumstances?	77	4	13	6
12. Did you ever drink before breakfast?	65	11	16	8
13. Did you ever drink things like hair tonic, rubbing alcohol, or other non-beverage alcohol?	86	2	6	6
14. Have you ever gone on benders?	66	8	11	15
15. Have you ever had memory losses (blackouts) when drinking?	69	10	11	10
16. Have you ever experienced impotence associated with drinking?	84	6	5	5
17. Have you ever had the shakes, seen or heard things that weren't there, had fits, had DT's, or had liver trouble associated with drinking?	74	6	15	5

(From Q. J. Stud. Alcohol 33: 111-116, 1972, copyright 1972 by J. Stud.
Alcohol, Inc., New Brunswick, N.J. 08903. Reprinted by permission.)

TABLE 18

"NO" ANSWERS AT 2ND INTERVIEW AMONG THOSE WITH "YES" ANSWERS AT 1ST INTERVIEW (45)

Total Number "Yes" Answers at 1st Interview	1-2 (N=35)		3-6 (N=50)		7-17 (N=38)		0-17 (N=176)	
	"Yes" Answers 1st Interv.	% "No" Answers 2nd Interv.	"Yes" Answers 1st Interv.	% "No" Answers 2nd Interv.	"Yes" Answers 1st Interv.	% "No" Answers 2nd Interv.	"Yes" Answers 1st Interv.	% "No" Answers 2nd Interv.
1. Has your family ever objected to your drinking?	21	62	41	37	34	21	96	36
2. Did you ever think you drank too much in general?	1	0	20	55	33	24	54	35
3. Have others, such as friends, physicians, clergymen, ever said you drank too much?	1	100	23	57	31	39	55	47
4. Have you ever felt guilty about drinking?	0	—	6	83	14	36	20	50
5. Have you ever lost friends because of drinking?	1	100	2	0	20	45	23	43
6. Did you ever get into trouble at work because of drinking?	0	—	4	75	15	33	19	42
7. Did you ever have trouble with driving because of drinking?	2	100	11	45	17	35	30	43
8. Have you ever been arrested for drinking or disturbing the peace?	5	60	27	41	29	21	61	33
9. Have you ever been in fights when drinking?	4	25	20	55	32	19	56	32

Total Number "Yes" Answers at 1st Interview

	1-2 (N=35)		3-6 (N=50)		7-17 (N=38)		0-17 (N=176)	
	"Yes" Answers 1st Interv.	% "No" Answers 2nd Interv.	"Yes" Answers 1st Interv.	% "No" Answers 2nd Interv.	"Yes" Answers 1st Interv.	% "No" Answers 2nd Interv.	"Yes" Answers 1st Interv.	% "No" Answers 2nd Interv.
10. Have you ever wanted to stop drinking but couldn't?	1	100	2	100	8	75	11	82
11. Have you ever tried to control your drinking by trying to drink only under certain circumstances?	0	—	3	100	14	50	17	59
12. Did you ever drink before breakfast?	7	14	7	72	20	40	34	41
13. Did you ever drink things like hair tonic, rubbing alcohol, nonbeverage alcohol?	3	100	5	80	6	67	14	79
14. Have you ever gone on benders?	1	0	13	85	26	58	40	65
15. Have you ever had memory losses (blackouts) when drinking?	0	—	11	64	25	44	36	50
16. Have you ever experienced impotence associated with drinking?	1	0	5	60	12	42	18	45
17. Have you ever had the shakes, seen or heard things that weren't there, had fits, had DT's, or had liver trouble associated with drinking?	0	—	3	100	17	35	20	45
Total	48	54	203	54	353	36	604	44

(From Q. J. Stud. Alcohol 33: 111-116, 1972, copyright 1972 by J. Stud. Alcohol, Inc., New Brunswick, N.J. 08903. Reprinted by permission.)

interview, a follow-up interview eight to nine years later will result in the same diagnosis in approximately three-quarters of the cases. Some subjects not considered alcoholic originally will warrant such a diagnosis at follow-up, suggesting that, with time, new cases of alcoholism will develop and other incipient cases will become more definite. Finally, one may expect a minority of subjects to be considered nonalcoholic at follow-up who had been considered alcoholics originally.

The inconsistencies between the two interviews probably resulted from several factors. Deliberate denial may have occurred in some cases, most likely those reporting 7 or more symptoms originally and none at follow-up. This seems an unlikely general explanation, however. Too many of the men who denied alcoholism symptoms at follow-up reported other possibly unflattering attributes (drug abuse, homosexuality, criminal behavior) to allow an inference that they tried to picture themselves in a more favorable light with regard to alcoholism. Further, the proportion who failed to receive a follow-up diagnosis of sociopathy, drug dependence, anxiety neurosis, or homosexuality after receiving one of these diagnoses originally was the same for the inconsistent as for the consistent alcoholics.

Nor were the inconsistencies likely to have been the result of interviewer bias. Six psychiatrists conducted the original and 9 the follow-up interviews. No particular interviewers were associated with inconsistencies, nor was there an apparent association between the interviewers' drinking practices and the inconsistencies. The inconsistencies did not result from differences in age at either interview or from differences in time spent in prison during the period of follow-up. Failure of memory and misunderstanding of question or answer probably accounted for some inconsistencies.

Nevertheless, the striking association between the number of alcoholism symptoms (probably reflecting extent and severity of alcoholism) and consistency points to what is probably the most important factor. The more extensive the original drinking problem, the more likely the subject is to be consistent in his answers to each question at follow-up. Conversely, the milder or more borderline the alcoholism, the greater the inconsistency. The increased percentage of blacks among inconsistent subjects probably reflects the fact that the average number of alcoholism symptoms reported at the first interview by blacks was smaller than that reported by whites (2.3 versus 4.1, p<.01).

The diagnosis of alcoholism was more consistent than the reporting of individual symptoms: 73 percent of the diagnoses were confirmed (Table 16) compared to 56 percent of the individual symptoms (Table 19). This suggests that, though an alcoholic may be inconsistent in reporting an individual symptom, even when he denies a symptom at follow-up that he reported originally, he is likely to report some other symptom that will justify the diagnosis. This further suggests that the inconsistent history

TABLE 19
ANTISOCIAL MANIFESTATIONS REPORTED AT
THE FIRST INTERVIEW: MALE FELONS (44)

	"Consistent" Antisocial Personality N=92		"Inconsistent" Antisocial Personality N=38
School Delinquency, Any	86%		74%
Repeated truancy	73%	p<.001	32%
Expelled or suspended	41%		32%
Excessive Fighting, Any	78%		63%
Under age 18	55%		38%
Age 18 or older	59%	p<.02	34%
Before and after age 18	37%	p<.01	11%
Runaway Overnight	54%	p<.01	24%
Period of Aimless Wandering over Country (wanderlust)	36%		21%
Poor Work History	63%		50%
"Flat-Timer" Status (more extensive criminal career)	55%	p<.05	34%
Mean Number Prior Arrests	8.6	p<.001	5.6
Mean Number Prior Imprisonments	2.7	p<.05	1.8

(From Am. J. Psychiatry 128: 360-361, 1971, copyright 1971 by the American Psychiatric Association. Reprinted by permission.)

is not the result of deliberate denial. It also indicates the advantage of basing an alcoholism diagnosis on the presence of a number of symptoms rather than on any single pathognomonic manifestation.

Consistency in the Diagnosis of Sociopathy

Ninety-two men received the diagnosis of sociopathy at both interviews (the "consistent" group) and 38 men received this diagnosis at the first interview but not at follow-up because they denied manifestations they had reported originally (the "inconsistent" group).

Responses from the first interview to questions dealing with antisocial and delinquent behavior were compared to see whether the two groups differed with regard to the frequency of such manifestations. The results are summarized in Table 19. They indicate that the consistent subjects reported more antisocial, delinquent, and criminal behavior at the first interview than did the inconsistent subjects. This was true for each item of behavior. For example, for consistent subjects the mean number of prior arrests was 8.6; for inconsistent subjects it was 5.6, $p<.001$. The mean number of prior imprisonments for consistent subjects was 2.7; for inconsistent subjects it was 1.8, $p<.05$.

The results contradict the simple assumption that antisocial individuals are untrustworthy historians. The more severe and extensive the original history of delinquent, antisocial, and criminal behavior, the more consistent was the history of this behavior at follow-up. While it is possible, and even probable, that some inconsistency resulted from deliberate efforts to mislead, this is probably not the major explanation. Many men, for example, who denied at follow-up a symptom they had reported at the first interview, told other unflattering things about themselves, making it unreasonable to conclude that they were simply trying to present themselves in a more favorable light.

Misunderstanding or failure of memory can produce an incorrect score on any individual item. More importantly, a person who at the initial interview reported many symptoms was more likely than one who reported few symptoms to repeat enough of them at follow-up to again receive a diagnosis of sociopathy. Again, support for this conclusion came from an examination of racial differences. Half the inconsistent cases of sociopathy were black compared to 19 percent of the consistent cases (p<.001). The probable explanation for this is that white subjects reported each symptom in Table 19 more frequently than black subjects.

The findings for sociopathy parallel those for alcoholism. Diagnostic consistency in these disorders is related to their initial extent and severity. Subjects with more extensive and severe disorders are more likely to report a consistent history at follow-up.

EIGHT-TO-NINE-YEAR FOLLOW-UP:
CRIMINAL RECIDIVISM (37, 47)

Six measures of recidivism were used: the percent rearrested, reimprisoned, and reconvicted of a felony, at least once and more than once for each criterion.

Recidivism rates were based upon information obtained from the men at follow-up because it was not possible to get up-to-date FBI reports, and the available police and prison records were not equally complete for each man. There is evidence, however, that the men reported more arrests and imprisonments than were contained in the FBI reports. At the eight-to-nine-year follow-up interviews, the men reported 975 arrests and 486 imprisonments up to the time of three-year follow-up FBI reports (see above). The corresponding figures from the FBI reports were 926 arrests and 404 imprisonments.

Since the distribution of psychiatric diagnoses varied somewhat between the original and follow-up studies, recidivism rates were calculated for each diagnosis at each interview. In addition, recidivism rates were calculated for active and remitted alcoholism and drug dependence. Remitted alcoholism or drug dependence were the diagnoses for subjects who had either stopped drinking or abusing drugs for at least two years before the follow-up interview or whose drinking or drug abuse had moderated to the extent that they had experienced no social, psychological, or medical complications for at least two years before the follow-up interview.

Recidivism rates for the entire sample were very high (Table 20). Eighty-five percent were rearrested at least once, 62 percent more than once. Nearly half were reimprisoned at least once, almost a quarter more than once. Over two-fifths were reconvicted of a felony at least once, more than a sixth more than once.

Flat-timer status, relative youth (under age 40), sociopathy, alcoholism (particularly active alcoholism), and drug dependence (opiates, barbiturates, and amphetamines) were all associated with one or more increased recidivism rates.

None of the differences between whites and blacks was statistically significant.

Because of the striking differences in recidivism associated with criminal status (parolee vs. flat-timer) and age, recidivism rates were calculated separately for all parolees, for all flat-timers, for parolees under age 40, and for flat-timers under age 40. The number of subjects aged 40 or older was too small for further separate analysis.

There were 120 comparisons between parolees and flat-timers controlling for age, race, and the presence or absence of each psychiatric diagnosis at each interview. The flat-timers' recidivism rate exceeded that of the parolees in 108 of the comparisons. Of these, 47 were statistically significant. The age differences observed for the entire sample were also noted for the parolees and flat-timers separately. Each of the 12 comparisons (6 recidivism measures for each criminal status) revealed higher rates for subjects under age 40; 5 were statistically significant.

Similarly, the diagnoses of sociopathy, alcoholism, and drug dependence were associated with increased recidivism rates when all parolees, all flat-timers, parolees under 40, and flat-timers under 40 were analyzed separately. The diagnosis of sociopathy was associated with higher recidivism rates in 45 of the 48 possible comparisons between those with and without the diagnosis in these 4 groups; 3 were statistically significant. The diagnosis of alcoholism was associated with higher rates in 40 of the 48 com-

TABLE 20

CRIMINAL RECIDIVISM RATES: 8-9-YEAR FOLLOW-UP:
TOTAL SAMPLE MALE FELONS (47)

	N	Rearrested		Reimprisoned		Reconvicted of a Felony	
		At Least Once %	More Than Once %	At Least Once %	More Than Once %	At Least Once %	More Than Once %
Total	176	85	62	49	24	41	17
1st Interview:							
Parolee	94	80	53	33	14	27	8
Flat-timer	82	90	72*	67‡	35†	59‡	27†
White	125	84	62	49	24	42	16
Black	51	86	61	49	23	39	20
1st Interview:							
Age <40	156	89	68	53	27	46	19
Age ≧40	20	50‡	15‡	10‡	0*	10†	0
1st Interview:							
Sociopathy +§	137	86	64	53	26	46	20
0	39	80	54	36	15	26*	8
2nd Interview:							
Sociopathy +§	106	89	66	64	30	54	25
0	70	79	56	31‡	14*	23‡	7†
1st Interview:							
Alcoholism +§	91	87	68	56	35	45	22
0	85	82	55	41	14†	38	10
2nd Interview:							
Alcoholism +§	93	88	70	49	31	39	18
0	83	81	53*	48	16*	45	16
2nd Interview:							
Alcoholism							
Active§	55	98	84	67	47	49	27
Remitted§	38	74†	50†	24‡	8‡	24*	5*
1st Interview:							
Drug Dependence +§	15	93	80	67	60	60	53
0	161	84	60	47	20†	40	14‡
2nd Interview:							
Drug Dependence +§	26	92	69	69	42	62	42
0	150	83	61	45*	21*	38*	13‡
2nd Interview:							
Drug Dependence							
Active§	13	100	85	77	62	77	62
Remitted§	13	85	54	61	23	46	23

* p<.05
† p<.01
‡ p<.001
§ Includes definite and questionable cases.

(From Am. J. Psychiatry *127*: 832-835, 1970, copyright 1970 by the American Psychiatric Association. Reprinted by permission.)

parisons; 7 were statistically significant. The diagnosis of drug dependence was associated with higher rates in 40 of the 48 comparisons; 4 were statistically significant.

The diagnosis of active alcoholism was associated with higher rates than the diagnosis of remitted alcoholism in each of the 24 comparisons made; 12 were statistically significant. Finally, the diagnosis of active drug dependence was associated with higher rates than the diagnosis of remitted drug dependence in 20 of the 24 comparisons made; 4 were statistically significant.

To recapitulate, a more extensive criminal career, relative youth, sociopathy, alcoholism, and drug dependence were all associated with increased rates of criminal recidivism. These variables apparently predict criminal recidivism; each variable at the first interview was associated with one or more significantly increased recidivism rates at follow-up.

The two factors most closely associated with recidivism were age and extent of prior criminal behavior reflected in parolee or flat-timer status. The increased recidivism risk associated with the diagnosis of sociopathy may simply be an extension of the latter factor since the diagnosis is based on a history of recurrent delinquency and antisocial behavior that characteristically begins in childhood or adolescence and usually antedates serious police trouble.

The lower recidivism rates for subjects age 40 or older is consistent with the general view that crime is a manifestation of youth. Age and extent of the prior criminal career apparently summate in their effect upon recidivism rates. Rearrest varied from 56 percent for parolees age 40 or older to 94 percent for flat-timers under 40, reimprisonment varied between 6 percent and 69 percent, and reconviction of a felony between 6 percent and 60 percent.

The increased recidivism rates after prolonged follow-up associated with sociopathy, alcoholism, and drug dependence further indicate that these disorders are related to criminality. The differences between active and remitted forms of alcoholism and drug dependence indicate that these disorders play important roles in aggravating sociopathic and criminal tendencies.

The absence of significant racial differences in recidivism warrants comment, since at the three-year follow-up there was an increased rearrest rate for blacks. As noted above, however, the absence of a parallel increased reimprisonment rate probably indicated only that blacks were more vulnerable to arrests for "suspicion." The equally high rearrest rates for whites and blacks at the eight-to-nine-year follow-up suggest that black and white recidivists differ principally in that blacks are likely to be rearrested sooner. There were no differences in the more important measures of reimprisonment and repeat felony conviction.

The overall results present a pessimistic picture. Nearly half the men under age 40 were reconvicted of a felony, and almost 20 percent were reconvicted more than once. Although youth, sociopathy, alcoholism, and drug dependence are highly correlated with recidivism, rearrest and reimprisonment may occur even when these features are absent.

STUDY OF WIVES OF CONVICTED MALE FELONS (48)

Table 21 presents data comparing psychiatric family history and parental home experience of the wives and men interviewed at follow-up. For the men, findings from the original interviews were combined with those from the follow-up interviews. The men and women clearly came from similar families and home situations. Their family backgrounds were characterized by instability, parental discord, broken homes, alcoholism, criminality, frequent suicides and suicide attempts, and frequent psychiatric hospitalization.

Table 22 compares the prevalence of psychiatric disorders among wives with their husbands' first-degree female relatives. Again, great similarity is evident. Sociopathy, alcoholism, and hysteria were seen frequently in both groups. Fifteen percent of the wives and 11 percent of the female relatives received at least one of these diagnoses. Eleven percent of the wives and 6 percent of the female relatives received a diagnosis of either so-

81

Criminality and Psychiatric Disorders

TABLE 21

PSYCHIATRIC FAMILY HISTORY AND CHARACTERISTICS OF
PARENTAL HOME MALE FELONS AND THEIR WIVES (48)

	Wives N = 116 %	Men N = 176 %
Family History* Positive for		
Nervousness	41	36
"Nervous Breakdown"	25	19
Suicide	3	6
Attempted Suicide	9	7
Alcoholism	45	53
General Hospital for Alcoholism	12	14
Psychiatric Hospitalization	17	17
Prison or Jail	36	52
History of Parental Separation†	25	38
History of Parental Divorce	31	37
Father (or Surrogate): Drinking Problem	32	37
Cruel to Family	10	9
Prison or Jail	13	20
Not a Steady Worker	12	13
Neglected Family	14	9
Mother (or Surrogate): Drinking Problem	7	5
Cruel to Family	2	4
Prison or Jail	1	<1
Neglected Family	3	3
History of Living in Foster Home	2	8
in Orphan's Home	3	6
with relatives or friends	15	33

* Includes first- and second degree relatives.
† A separation was counted only if it did not lead to divorce, or if a recon-
ciliation took place before a later divorce. There were only a small number
of these latter situations, so that adding the figures for separation and divorce
closely approximates the percent separated *or* divorced.

(From Am. J. Psychiatry *126:* 1773-1776, 1970, copyright 1970 by the
American Psychiatric Association. Reprinted by permission.)

ciopathy or alcoholism. Slightly over 40 percent of each group
received a psychiatric diagnosis.

Table 23 summarizes the history of police trouble reported by
the wives and female relatives. The arrest history for female relatives is broken down into traffic arrests and nontraffic arrests. The

82

TABLE 22
PSYCHIATRIC DIAGNOSES IN WIVES AND FEMALE
RELATIVES (48)

Diagnosis	Wives (N=116) Percent	First Degree Female Relative (N=158) Percent
Anxiety Neurosis	14	10
Hysteria		
Definite	3	4
Probable	1	1
Total	4	5
Obsessional Neurosis	0	0
Schizophrenia	<1	0
Primary Affective Disorder	2	1
Organic Brain Syndrome	0	0
Sociopathy		
Definite	3	2
Questionable	3	1
Total	6	3
Alcoholism		
Definite	4	2
Questionable	3	3
Total	7	5
Drug Dependence	0	0
Homosexuality		
Significant	0	0
Any	0	0
Undiagnosed	15	25
History of Psychiatric Hospitalization	3	3
History of Suicide Attempt	7	1
Any Psychiatric Diagnosis	41	42

(From Am. J. Psychiatry 126: 1773-1776, 1970, copyright 1970 by the American Psychiatric Association. Reprinted by permission.)

figure for all of these arrests combined would be between 8 and 16 percent. The arrest history for the wives was not broken down in this way; the 18 percent includes both types of arrests. An unusually high rate of police trouble was reported by both groups

More than 40 percent of both wives and male felons had been

TABLE 23
HISTORY OF POLICE TROUBLE IN WIVES AND
FEMALE RELATIVES (48)

	Wives N = 116 %	First Degree Female Relative N = 158 %
History of Arrests: Traffic	—	8
Nontraffic	—	8
Total	18	between 8 and 16
History of Prison or Jail	3	3
History of Felony Conviction	3	1

(From Am. J. Psychiatry *126:* 1773-1776, 1970, copyright 1970 by the American Psychiatric Association. Reprinted by permission.)

married at least once before. Nearly all the previous marriages had ended in divorce rather than in death of spouse. About a quarter of the most recent or current marriages had ended in divorce or separation.

To summarize, convicted felons, the great majority of whom came from grossly disturbed families, married women from similar backgrounds. Their wives and first-degree female relatives revealed the same psychopathology. Thus, assortative, or nonrandom, mating, in which individuals from similar backgrounds tend to marry more often than would be expected by chance, was clearly evident. It suggests that children of these matings will be exposed to a double dose of factors that predispose to delinquency, sociopathy, criminality, alcoholism, and drug dependence—whether these factors are genetic, environmental, or both.

FIVE
Female Felons

INDEX STUDY (12, 13)

Age, Race, and Education

When originally studied, the female felons ranged in age from 17 to 54 years, with a mean of 27. Three-quarters were between 20 and 35.

Thirty-four were white, 30 were black, one was an American Indian, and one was of mixed background (American Indian and white).

Eleven women had not finished elementary school. Eight terminated their education after the eighth grade. Twenty-nine dropped out of high school. Seven graduated from high school without continuing further. Ten had attended some college without obtaining a degree, and one had graduated from college.

Job and Marital Histories

More than half of the women were unemployed, and a third were on welfare. Thirty percent were working in unskilled jobs. When they did work, nearly 75 percent had worked at unskilled jobs only, even though 41 percent had attended technical training programs, usually while in prison. The usual job of 35 percent was in the health field where most worked as nurse assistants.

Twenty percent of the women had never been married; all of these were under age 30. Twenty-two women had married before age 18. Twelve women had lived in common-law relationships for two years or more, and all of these had also been legally married to another man at some time. Among the 53 women who had ever been married, 23 had been divorced at least once. Nine had been divorced twice, and 3 women had been divorced three times. Twenty-one women had been separated, but not divorced. Thus, divorce or separation was reported by 83 percent of those ever married. At the time of the interview, 33 women were divorced or separated, 6 were widows, and 14 were living with a husband.

Index Crimes and Criminal History

The index crimes are listed in Table 24. The most frequent crime was homicide; crimes against persons (homicide, robbery, and assault) were the index crimes for 32 percent of the women.

Only 44 percent of the women had never been arrested or convicted prior to the index crime. Half had served at least one prior prison term and 3 women had served two separate prior prison terms. Twenty percent had a prior felony conviction.

Psychiatric Diagnoses

Table 25 summarizes the psychiatric diagnoses. Each woman received at least one diagnosis. Eighteen received only one diagnosis: 6 cases of hysteria, 4 cases of sociopathy, one case each of anxiety neurosis, depression, and questionable mental deficiency, and 5 cases with an undiagnosed psychiatric disorder (see below). The other women received more than one diagnosis. Altogether, there were 146 diagnoses, excluding casual homosexuality. Sociopathy, alcoholism, or drug dependence represented

TABLE 24
THE INDEX CRIME: FEMALE FELONS (12)

Crime	Number
Homicide	14
Shoplifting	11
Check Forgery*	11
Drug Violation†	10
Burglary	8
Robbery	5
Auto Theft	1
Embezzlement	3
Assault	2
Driving While Intoxicated	1

* One subject arrested on suspicion of murder, but convicted of check forgery.
† One subject arrested for sale of opiates but allowed to plead guilty of peace disturbance.

(From Am. J. Psychiatry 127: 303-311, 1970, copyright 1970 by the American Psychiatric Association. Reprinted by permission.)

62 percent of the diagnoses; the diagnosis of hysteria or significant homosexuality was made in another 31, or 21 percent. These 5 diagnoses comprised about 83 percent of all the psychiatric diagnoses.

Sociopathy. The most frequent diagnosis, seen in 65 percent of the women, was sociopathy. It was usually associated with other diagnoses: alcoholism in 60 percent, hysteria in 40 percent, drug dependence in 30 percent, casual or significant homosexuality in 28 percent, and anxiety neurosis in 14 percent. Uncomplicated sociopathy was seen in 19 percent. Seventy percent of the sociopaths received additional diagnosis of alcoholism or drug dependence.

The antisocial symptoms began on the average between age 11 and 12. Prior felony convictions were found exclusively among the sociopaths, of whom 26 percent gave such a history. The index offense was the first arrest for 23 percent of the sociopaths compared to 78 percent of the nonsociopaths.

TABLE 25

PSYCHIATRIC DIAGNOSES: FEMALE FELONS (12)

Diagnosis	Number of Cases	Percent
Sociopathy		
definite	39	
questionable	4	
Total	43	65
Alcoholism		
definite	28	
questionable	3	
Total	31	47
Hysteria		
definite	25	
probable	2	
Total	27	41
Drug Dependence		
definite	16	
questionable	1	
Total	17	26
Homosexuality		
significant	4	6
casual	5	
Total	9	14
Anxiety Neurosis		
without other diagnosis	1	
Total	7	11
Depression		
definite	0	
probable	1	
Total	1	1
Mental Deficiency		
IQ 60	1	
questionable (no IQ test result)	3	
Total	4	6
Schizophrenia		
Total	1	1.5
Undiagnosed		
Total	8	12

(Slightly modified from Am. J. Psychiatry *127*: 303-311, 1970, copyright 1970 by The American Psychiatric Association. Reprinted by permission.)

Alcoholism. The next most frequent diagnosis was alcoholism, seen in 47 percent. No woman, however, received a diagnosis of alcoholism without some other diagnosis in addition. Ninety-three percent of the alcoholics were either sociopaths or hysterics as well. A third of the alcoholics were also drug dependent.

Heavy drinking began between the ages of 12 and 50, with a median of 19. Two-thirds began between age 16 and 22. In 5 cases (4 definite and one questionable), the alcoholism was in remission. At the time of the index crime, there were 20 active alcoholics. Eight of these had been intoxicated during the offense. In addition, 4 of the 35 nonalcoholic women had also been intoxicated at the time of the index offense.

Problem drinking, defined as reporting any of the symptoms of alcoholism, whether or not the full diagnostic criteria were fulfilled, was reported by 34 women, over half.

Hysteria. There were 27 women with hysteria, or 41 percent. Three of the 10 nonsociopathic hysterics were alcoholics, and one was drug dependent.

Nearly half of the women with hysteria reported "always" having had one or another of the diagnostic symptoms. All cases of hysteria had begun by the time of menarche. Antisocial symptoms began after hysterical symptoms in two-thirds of those receiving both diagnoses. In the remainder, the two disorders apparently began simultaneously.

Histrionic personality features (dramatic overstatement, seductive and manipulative behavior, ostentatious grooming and dress) were seen in 60 percent of the hysterics.

Drug Dependence. This diagnosis was applied in cases where the use of heroin, amphetamines, barbiturates, cocaine, or LSD, alone or in combination with each other or with marihuana, but not marihuana alone, was involved. Drug dependence was found in 26 percent of the women. It was seen in 30 percent of the sociopaths and 17 percent of the others. Alcoholism was seen in 59 percent of those with drug dependence.

The median age of onset of drug abuse was 19, with a range

from 14 to 42 years. Multiple drug abuse was characteristic, particularly among sociopaths. A quarter of those with drug dependence apparently were in remission. Nearly another quarter of the entire sample reported experimenting with drugs without becoming dependent. Altogether, nearly half of the women reported drug experimentation or drug dependence. Twenty-nine percent of the women were using drugs at the time of the index crime. Forty-four percent of the entire sample were intoxicated by drugs, alcohol, or both, at the time of the index crime. Fourteen percent had committed the index crime to get money for drugs (or alcohol).

Homosexuality. Nine women reported some overt homosexual experience. In 5 cases, it was limited to the time in prison.

Four women (2 alcoholic sociopaths, one drug-dependent sociopath, and one drug-dependent alcoholic) were significantly homosexual; 3 preferred homosexual relationships, and one regarded herself as bisexual. Homosexual fantasy and sex play began early in 2 cases: one at age 5 and another at age 7. Each of these women had been disturbed by her homosexual tendencies during adolescence, and one had sought psychiatric help. One of the 4 had never married; the other 3 had been separated from their husbands for long periods. Three reported heterosexual prostitution. Three reported heterosexual frigidity but were orgasmic homosexually. None reported an exclusively active or passive role.

The five women with only casual homosexuality were all sociopaths. Only 2 of them reported homosexual relations outside of prison.

Anxiety Neurosis. Anxiety neurosis was seen in 11 percent. In one case, it was the only diagnosis; in another, the only other diagnosis was questionable sociopathy. In the remaining cases, the anxiety symptoms were secondary to sociopathy or alcoholism.

Depression. Only one case with a probable primary depression was seen. Several women gave histories of secondary depressions, however. Most of these were hysterics for whom separate diagnoses of secondary depression were not made. A definite secondary depression was seen in one drug-dependent woman, and probable secondary depressions were seen in 2 women who each received diagnoses of sociopathy, alcoholism, and drug dependence.

Mental Deficiency. Intellectual function was estimated on the basis of school history, mental status examination, and, where available, I.Q. tests. Four subjects were considered mildly retarded, although none severely enough to interfere with daily life. Mental deficiency was the only diagnosis in one case. Two others were sociopaths; alcoholism and hysteria were present in one of these women. The fourth woman was also schizophrenic. None of the 4 had completed elementary school; 3 were illiterate.

Schizophrenia. Schizophrenia was seen in only one case. She was also questionably mentally deficient (see above).

Undiagnosed. Five women were psychiatrically ill but failed to meet the criteria for any of the above diagnoses. In 2, the clinical histories suggested hysteria. One of these women had been psychiatrically hospitalized earlier. She had received a diagnosis of Ganser syndrome (30) on the basis of approximate, ridiculous, and inconsistent answers.

In 3 women the undiagnosed manifestations complicated other diagnoses: alcoholism in one woman (with a picture suggesting hysteria), sociopathy, alcoholism, and amphetamine abuse in a second (with a picture that could have been drug intoxication, mania, or schizophrenia), and sociopathy with hysteria in a third (with a picture that may have been early schizophrenia).

Confirmation of Diagnoses

The validity of information obtained at interview may be questioned in any study. In a study of criminals, this question is particularly likely to arise. Fortunately, extensive data from other sources were available for each woman. These data, independently and routinely assembled by parole officers, included court records, police reports, prison records, social history of the family, and information about schooling, jobs, marriages, military service, and health. The data were recorded in presentencing reports and in progress reports to the courts concerning parole status. Additional records were also obtained from hospitals, clinics, and private physicians. All of these records were reviewed for comments and observations that might pertain to the following diagnoses: sociopathy, alcoholism, drug dependence, homosexuality, and hysteria.

Sociopathy. Table 26 summarizes outside data concerning childhood and adolescent difficulties pertinent to the diagnosis of sociopathy, comparing women who received this diagnosis to those who did not. The findings indicate that the diagnosis of sociopathy identified those who had previously demonstrated the characteristic manifestations of sociopathy.

Alcoholism. Serious drinking problems were noted in outside records of 12, or 39 percent, of the 31 women who were considered to be alcoholic at interview. The records of the women who were not considered to be alcoholic at interview failed to indicate any drinking problems. Thus, the diagnostic criteria identified all with independent evidence of drinking problems; i.e., no case of alcoholism identified independently was missed.

Drug Dependence. Outside records indicated drug dependence in 13, or 77 percent, of the 17 women with this diagnosis at interview, and failed to indicate drug dependence in the women who were not considered drug dependent at interview. Again, the diagnostic criteria correctly identified all with independent evidence of drug abuse problems.

Homosexuality. Significant homosexuality was confirmed in the records of 3 of the 4 women who received this diagnosis at interview, and casual homosexuality was confirmed in the records of 3 of the 5 women so diagnosed at interview. In addition, outside

TABLE 26

RECORD INFORMATION CONCERNING CHILDHOOD AND
ADOLESCENT BEHAVIOR (BEFORE AGE 18):
FEMALE FELONS (12)

	Sociopaths N = 43 %	Nonsociopaths N = 23 %
Juvenile arrests—total	54	0
Runaway	42	0
Fighting	16	0
Incorrigible	14	0
Theft	7	1*
Sexual Immorality	9	0
Late after Curfew	5	0
Peace Disturbance	7	0
Reform School	32	0
Out Late or Truant with Male Companion	35	9
Sexual Misconduct—total	65	26
Arrest for Sexual Immorality	9	0
Prostitution	7	0
Venereal Disease	9	0
Incest	5	4
Homosexuality	9	0
Illegitimate Pregnancy	35	22
Marriage before 18	40	22
to Sociopath or Alcoholic	37	13
Quit School Pregnant	23	17
History of Rape or Molestation	19	4
Required Psychiatric Attention	14	4

* One case reported she was caught shoplifting at age 14 and talked to a juvenile officer but was not charged.

(From Am. J. Psychiatry *127:* 303-311, 1970, copyright 1970 by The American Psychiatric Association. Reprinted by permission.)

records indicated significant homosexuality in one woman and casual homosexuality in 3 women among the 57 who denied all homosexuality at interview. Thus, two-thirds of the interview diagnoses were confirmed, and 4 additional cases of homosexual behavior were identified from the records. The interview picked up 6 of the 10 women identified independently as showing homosexual behavior: 3 of the 4 significant homosexuals and 3 of the 6 with casual homosexuality.

Hysteria. Prison records were available for 29 women. A comparison between those who received a diagnosis of hysteria and those who did not is presented in Table 27. The data indicate that, when in prison, the former were much more likely to display clinical manifestations consistent with hysteria. Table 28 presents a similar comparison with regard to information obtained from other hospitals, clinics, and physicians. Again, women with hysteria had presented the characteristic clinical manifestations to other physicians and clinical facilities. The 27 women with hysteria reported 116 hospitalizations, or, 4.3 per women. Confirmation of 93 hospitalizations was obtained. All but 2 of the 27 women with hysteria had been hospitalized at least once. The 37 nonhysterics reported only 1.6 hospitalizations per woman, and

TABLE 27

MEDICAL INFORMATION FROM PRISON RECORDS: FEMALE FELONS (12)

	Hysteria N = 13 %	Not Hysteria N = 19 %
Nervousness Requiring Medication	77	21
Excessive Clinic Visits (unexplained symptoms in 3 or more organ systems per year or doctor's statement that visits were "excessive")	62	0
Frequent Somatic Complaints to nonmedical personnel (e.g., "constantly complains of every ailment known to man")	46	0
Nonpsychiatric Hospitalization during prison term	31	5
Psychiatric Hospitalization during prison term	15	5
At Least One of the Above	100	31
At Least Two of the Above	85	5

(From Am. J. Psychiatry *127*: 303-311, 1970, copyright 1970 by The American Psychiatric Association. Reprinted by permission.)

TABLE 28

MEDICAL INFORMATION FROM HOSPITALS, CLINICS,
AND PHYSICIANS: FEMALE FELONS (12)

	Hysteria N = 27 %	Not Hysteria N = 39 %
Classic Conversion Reactions	26	3
Other Unexplained Somatic Symptoms	52	8
Depression or Suicide Attempt	37	5
Hyperemesis Gravidarum	7	0
Diagnosis of Anxiety or Hysteria	30	5
At Least Two of the Above	45	7

(From Am. J. Psychciatry 127: 303-311, 1970, copyright 1970 by The American Psychiatric Association. Reprinted by permission.)

one-third had never been hospitalized. The data indicate that the diagnosis of hysteria at interview picked out those women who had previously and independently been identified as showing many of the diagnostic symptoms of hysteria.

Criminal Guilt and Psychiatric Diagnosis

Certain unanticipated differences were noted at interview between women with and without hysteria in regard to their views concerning guilt and treatment by police, courts, and prisons. Hysterics were much more likely to report complete innocence (67 versus 10 percent), offer extenuating circumstances to mitigate their guilt (30 versus 15 percent), claim illegal arrest (22 versus 3 percent), unfair trial (22 versus 7 percent), or cruel treatment in prison or while on parole (37 versus 7 percent).

Discussion

The prevalence of sociopathy, alcoholism, and drug dependence was similar to that among male felons, emphasizing again the significant association between these disorders and criminality.

The high prevalence of hysteria—more than 20 times greater

than the general population (103)—was striking. Even if all cases with additional diagnoses of sociopathy, alcoholism, or drug dependence were excluded, the prevalence of hysteria, 9 percent, was increased more than fourfold.

Sociopathy or hysteria was found in 80 percent of the female felons (regardless of other diagnoses): sociopathy alone, 39 percent; hysteria alone, 15 percent; and both, 26 percent. These results indicated a significant association between hysteria and sociopathy. They strongly suggest that at least some cases of hysteria and sociopathy share a common etiology or pathogenesis. Since hysteria is predominantly a disorder of women while sociopathy is predominantly a disorder of men, it was suggested that, depending upon the sex of the individual, the same etiologic and pathogenetic factors may lead to different, though sometimes overlapping, clinical pictures (12). This hypothesis was strengthened by the observation that hysteria and sociopathy are the two psychiatric disorders most often associated with classical conversion symptoms (38, 54).

The frequency of any homosexual experiences (casual or significant) of 20 percent (including cases identified by outside records) is probably higher than that of the general population corrected for age, education, and marital status. Kinsey and associates (63) found that the cumulative incidence of any homosexual experiences to orgasm for women in their late 20's who had not graduated from high school and who were separated, divorced, or widowed (the modal subject in this study) was less than 10 percent. On the other hand, the frequency of significant homosexuality (Kinsey grades 3 to 6), of 8 percent (including the one case identified solely by records) was not very different from the 6 to 7 percent Kinsey reported for previously married women in their early 20's. The latter figure was not controlled for education, however, and was derived from a study of white women only, so further comparison was not possible. Since all but one of the women with a history of homosexuality were sociopaths, the increased prevalence of casual homosexual behavior was probably simply a manifestation of sociopathy, evident particularly when the women were imprisoned.

As was true for the male criminals, the prevalence of anxiety neurosis, depression, mild mental deficiency, and schizophrenia, probably did not differ significantly from the general population rate. Three of the undiagnosed cases presented clinical features suggesting hysteria. If, in time, the full picture of hysteria were to develop, the association between criminality and hysteria would be further strengthened.

The confirmation of interview diagnoses by outside independent information indicates that even criminals will cooperate with a clinical study carried out under suitable medical auspices.

Finally, the differences between women with and without hysteria concerning claims of guilt, innocence, and injustice are not easily explained, though many clinicians undertaking psychotherapeutic management of women with hysteria have noted a tendency for these patients to blame their troubles on others. The observation may merely indicate that hysterics who are criminals continue to behave like other hysterics.

SOCIAL, FAMILIAL, AND PERSONAL BACKGROUNDS (13)

Socioeconomic Background

The head of the home in which the women had been raised was an unskilled laborer in 56 percent of the cases, semi-skilled or a clerical worker in 32 percent, and a professional or managerial worker in 12 percent. Twenty-one percent had been reared in a rural environment until adulthood.

Parental Home Experience

At least one parent permanently absent from the household before she reached age 18 was reported by 65 percent of the women. Parental loss included the father only in 30 percent, mother only in 8 percent, and both in 27 percent of the cases. Parental death was reported by 18 percent; parental divorce or separation by about half. Nine percent were illegitimate. One woman had been removed from her home by a welfare agency because of parental neglect.

Because of the high rate of parental loss, the women had been reared in a variety of settings. Over half had lived away from their parents for varying periods. Twenty-six percent had lived with relatives or friends, 14 percent had lived in foster homes or orphanages, and 15 percent had lived "on their own."

Reported parental antisocial behavior was frequent. The father, or surrogate, was reported as a heavy drinker by 53 percent of the women, as neglecting the family by 29 percent, as having been in prison or jail by 20 percent, as an erratic worker by 14 percent, and as cruel or physically abusive by 12 percent. Similarly, the mother, or surrogate, was said to have been a heavy drinker by 21 percent, to have been cruel or abusive by 12 percent, to have been in prison or jail by 9 percent, and to have neglected the family by 9 percent. On the basis of the family history, the biological father of 55 percent of the women received a diagnosis of suspected sociopathy or suspected alcoholism; the corresponding figure for the biological mother was 27 percent. More mothers than fathers, however, were considered to warrant some psychiatric diagnosis (76 percent versus 59 percent).

School History

In addition to their limited schooling, already described earlier (nearly three-quarters had failed to graduate from high school), 14 women (nearly a quarter) quit school because of pregnancy. Expulsion or suspension from school was reported by 33 percent, repeated truancy was reported by 32 percent, repeated fights in school leading to trouble with teachers was reported by 36 percent, and having to see the principal by 52 percent. Parents had been required to come to school for academic or disciplinary reasons in 33 percent.

Mental deficiency was not frequent, but low academic achievement was common. Fifty-five percent of the women failed one or more subjects: 26 percent had to repeat a year of school. The 66 women attended a total of 271 primary and secondary schools. In addition to their formal academic education, 41 percent of the women had attended one or more technical training programs, often while in prison.

Work History

Forty-seven percent reported having been fired from a job for poor performance at least once. Seventy percent had quit a job without having another one to go to at least once. The 66 women reported 395 jobs in the last ten years, or 6 jobs per woman. Forty-two percent had never held a job for as long as one year. Sixty-five percent had never held a job for as long as two years.

Sexual History

The median age at first heterosexual intercourse was 16. Eight women reported being raped; 2 twice. In 4 cases, the offender was the victim's father (one case) or stepfather (3 cases). Other forms of incest were reported by 3 women.

More than a quarter of the women had been prostitutes. Over 20 percent had experienced venereal disease. Sexual inadequacy was reported by 79 percent: sexual indifference by 67 percent, frigidity by 52 percent, and dyspareunia by 36 percent.

Homosexual experiences were described earlier.

Relations with Husbands

Seventy-two percent of those ever married had been married at least once to a sociopath or alcoholic. Fighting with husbands or being beaten by them was reported by 64 percent of those ever married. Thirty-one women complained of their husbands' nonsupport. Twenty-three complained of their husbands' infidelity. On the other hand, 29 women reported being unfaithful to their husbands. In 30 of the 44 cases of separation or divorce, the women had left their husbands.

Pregnancy and Motherhood

Fifty-five of the women had been pregnant at least once, and 51 had given birth to at least one child, for a total of 144 children. Nineteen of the children had died: 6 were stillborn, 7 others died in the first year, and 6 more died before age 3. Ten women reported 17 abortions: 16 spontaneous and one illegal. Forty percent of the children were conceived out of wedlock. Thirty-one women reported at least one illegitimate pregnancy.

Nine women had been declared "unfit mothers" by the court; 4 of these had been convicted of child abuse. Three had been required by the court to give up their children for adoption. Two other women voluntarily placed their children for adoption. Altogether, 10 children had been placed for adoption. The children of another 21 women lived with relatives (36 children). A total, then, of 46 children (37 percent of those alive) did not live with their mothers.

Religion

Thirty-five women were interested in religion; in 22 this began after their index conviction. Twenty-eight women reported frequent prayer, representing a recent change in 18. Twenty-three women read the Bible often; this was a recent change in 15. Ten women reported communicating with God and believed that they had actually talked with Him or received a message from Him. Six women were currently active in church organizations. Fifteen others attended church regularly. Twenty-five were affiliated with a church but seldom attended. Nineteen were uninterested, and one was actively antagonistic.

Other Features

Forty-five women reported repeated fighting or using a weapon in a fight. Twenty-six women reported running away from home overnight, and 15 women reported at least one period of wanderlust. Most of the women denied significant feelings of guilt, sinfulness, or worthlessness. Pathological lying characterized 10 women. Lack of close friends or any organization tie was reported by 19 women.

Histrionic personality traits (dramatic overstatement, seductive and manipulative behavior, ostentatious grooming and dress) were present in a third of all the women. Five women spontaneously described themselves as having a "split personality" or a "multiple personality." Circumscribed persecutory feelings of being specially watched, followed, or plotted against (as by the police) were reported by 7 women.

Aggravating Influences and the Index Crime

It has already been noted that 44 percent of the women were intoxicated (alcohol, drugs, or both) at the time of the index crime. Another important factor was the presence of accomplices. Thirty-seven women had an accomplice at the index crime; 16 had only male accomplices, 8 had only female accomplices, and 13 had both. Thus, male accomplices were present in 44 percent of all the crimes. Index property crimes (shoplifting, burglary, auto theft, check offenses, and embezzlement) more often involved an accomplice than did the other crimes (65 percent versus 35 percent, p<.05). Accomplices, intoxication, or both, were present in 82 percent of the crimes.

Jealousy or sex-related emotional stress, such as infidelity, was involved in 12 index offenses: 11 of the 14 homicides and one of the 2 cases of aggravated assault. There were 13 male victims and 3 female victims.

Discussion

The severe social and familial pathology is striking. While similarly disturbed social and family settings characterized male felons, the situation seemed to be worse among the women felons. From the home environment in which they were raised to the home environment they provided for their own children, the picture was disheartening.

CRIMINAL RECIDIVISM (14)

Between October 1971 and February 1972, detailed and systematic reports of arrests and convictions subsequent to the 1969 interview were obtained. The length of follow-up ranged from 27 to 32 months with a mean of 29 months.

During this time, 22 women, or 33 percent, were rearrested at least once, for a total of 81 arrests. The most frequent reason for rearrest was shoplifting; 9 women had 22 such arrests. Seven women were rearrested 13 times for drug violations. Four women were rearrested 12 times for fraud or forged checks. Six women were rearrested 9 times for parole violations. Three were rearrested 7 times for burglary. Four were rearrested 5 times for assault. One woman was rearrested 4 times for receiving stolen property. Two women were rearrested 3 times for brandishing a deadly weapon. Two women were rearrested once each for malicious destruction of property. Two women were each rearrested once for auto theft. One woman was rearrested once for armed robbery, and one was rearrested once for peace disturbance. The number of arrests per woman ranged up to 12; of those with at least one arrest, the mean number was 3.7.

Fourteen women had a total of 21 reconvictions, including 5 women returned to prison after parole revocation instead of being tried for new offenses. Reconviction was for shoplifting (8 times by 5 women), parole violations (5 times by 5 women), fraudulent checks (4 times by 3 women), flourishing a deadly weapon (3 times by 3 women), and receiving stolen property (one case). At least one reconviction was experienced by 21 percent. Rearrests were almost four times as frequent as reconvictions, but 64 percent of those rearrested were eventually reconvicted.

Recidivism and Prior Criminal Record

Recidivism rates were correlated with prior criminal records, length of time on parole, and type of index crime (Table 29). Arrests or convictions prior to the index crime were associated with significantly higher rearrest and reconviction rates. Rearrests

TABLE 29

RECIDIVISM AND CRIMINAL RECORD—FEMALE FELONS
27-32 MONTHS FOLLOW-UP (14)

	N	\%	Rearrested Mean Number Rearrests	\%	Reconvicted Mean Number Reconvictions
Total Sample	66	33	1.23	21	0.32
Prior to index crime:					
History of arrest	37	46*	1.92†	30	0.49*
No history of arrest	29	17	0.34	10	0.10
History of conviction	13	62*	2.38	38	0.69*
No history of conviction	53	26	0.94	17	0.23
Index crimes:					
Robbery	5	80*	2.80	60*	0.60
Shoplifting	11	55	1.90	36	0.64
Burglary	8	50	1.13	25	0.25
Check forgery	11	27	1.73	27	0.64
Drug violation	10	30	1.40	10	0.30
Homicide	14	14	0.29	7	0.07
Embezzlement	3	0	0	0	0
Assault	2	0	0	0	0
Auto theft	1	0	0	0	0
Driving while intoxicated	1	0	0	0	0
Length of parole supervision prior to initial interview:					
Less than 1 month	10	80†	4.20† ⎤	70†	1.00 ⎤
1-23 months	48	29	0.81 ⎬§	15	0.23 ⎬‡
24 months or more	8	0*	0* ⎦	0	0 ⎦

* Difference between subgroup and all others significant at p<.05 level.
† Difference between subgroup and all others significant at p<.01 level.
‡ Correlation coefficient significant at p<.05 level.
§ Correlation coefficient significant at p<.01 level.

(From Arch. Gen. Psychiatry 29: 266-269, 1973, copyright 1973 by The American Medical Association. Reprinted by permission.)

and reconvictions were negatively correlated with the length of time on parole prior to the initial interview. The 5 robbers had the highest recidivism rates. This was the only index crime with significantly different rates at follow-up.

Recidivism and Prior Personal and Social History

Relative youth (under age 30), not completing the last level of school (grade school, high school, or college) in which enrolled, and never having married were associated with significantly higher recidivism rates (Table 30). The women who had never married were all under age 30; thus, it was not possible to compare recidivism in this group according to age and marital status separately. Among the 53 women who had married, the 27 under age 30 were more often recidivists than the others (37 percent versus 19 percent), but the difference was not significant.

TABLE 30

RECIDIVISM AND SELECTED DEMOGRAPHIC VARIABLES— FEMALE FELONS 27-32 MONTHS FOLLOW-UP (14)

Sample	N	Rearrested		Reconvicted	
		%	Mean Number	%	Mean Number
<Age 30	40	43*	1.68	30*	0.45
≦Age 30	26	19	0.54	8	0.12
White	36	31	1.31	19	0.31
Black	30	37	1.13	23	0.33
Education:					
8 years or less	19	26	0.95	16	0.21
9-11 years	29	52†	2.03*	34*	0.55
12 years or more	18	11	0.22	6	0.06
Did not finish last					
level entered	41	49†	1.93*	26	0.49
Marital status:					
Never married	13	54	1.85	46*	0.62
Living with husband	14	14	0.14	7	0.07
Separated or divorced	33	33	1.39	18	0.30
Widow	6	33	1.50	17	0.33
Employed at interview	33	27	0.76	21	0.27
Unemployed at interview	33	39	1.70	21	0.39

* Difference between subgroup and all others significant at $p < .05$ level.
† Difference between subgroup and all others significant at $p < .01$ level.

(From Arch. Gen. Psychiatry 29: 266-269, 1973, copyright 1973 by The American Medical Association. Reprinted by permission.)

Recidivism and Family History

The effect on recidivism of the following items of family history and early life experience were analyzed: parental divorce or separation, rearing by nonparents, first-degree relative in jail, father sociopathic, father alcoholic, mother sociopathic, and mother alcoholic. The 11 women whose father was sociopathic were more often rearrested compared to the other women (55 percent versus 29 percent, p<.05); their reconviction rate was also twice as high (36 percent versus 18 percent), but the difference was not significant. The other items were not associated with significantly different recidivism rates.

Recidivism and Psychiatric Diagnosis

Recidivism rates were positively associated with the following diagnoses, all made at the time of original study: sociopathy, drug dependence, and any homosexual behavior (Table 31). The data were analyzed further to evaluate the impact of these disorders separately.

All but one of the women with a history of homosexuality were also sociopaths; it was not possible, therefore, to compare the recidivism of the one nonsociopathic homosexual with the others. Among the 53 women with no history of homosexuality, recidivism was still significantly increased among the drug dependent and the sociopaths.

Stratification by the presence or absence of sociopathy and drug dependence separately resulted in cells too small for appropriate analysis. Nevertheless, women with sociopathy plus drug dependence had significantly higher recidivism rates than women with either disorder only.

Recidivism Among Sociopaths

Since 93 percent of the reconvicted women were sociopaths, but only 30 percent of the sociopaths were reconvicted, recidivism rates were re-examined for the sociopaths alone. Because there

TABLE 31

RECIDIVISM AND PSYCHIATRIC DIAGNOSIS—FEMALE FELONS
27-32 MONTHS FOLLOW-UP (14)

	N	Rearrested		Reconvicted	
		%	Mean Number	%	Mean Number
Total sample	66	33	1.23	21	0.32
Sociopathy	43	44*	1.79†	30*	0.47*
Alcoholism	31	39	1.61	23	0.35
Hysteria	27	26	1.22	19	0.26
Drug Dependence	17	71†	3.29‡	47†	0.76†
Homosexuality					
Significant	5	60	1.60	40	0.60
Any	13	62*	2.77†	38	0.69*
Anxiety Neurosis	7	43	1.43	29	0.57
Depression	4	50	1.00	50	0.50

* Difference between subgroup and all others significant at p<.05 level.
† Difference between subgroup and all others significant at p<.01 level.
‡ Difference between subgroup and all others significant at p<.001 level.

(From Arch. Gen. Psychiatry 29: 266-269, 1973, copyright 1973 by The American Medical Association. Reprinted by permission.)

were few nonsociopaths, and their recidivism rates were low, a separate analysis of these women was not useful. Among the sociopaths, recidivism rates were compared in relation to each of the personal, social, family history, and prior criminal record factors noted above. Drug dependence, age, and marital status were the only significant differences between recidivist and non-recidivist sociopaths.

Drug dependence was significantly more frequent among the 19 arrested sociopaths than among the other 24 (58 percent versus 8 percent, p<.01) and more frequent among the 13 convicted sociopaths than among the other 30 (62 percent versus 17 percent, p<.01).

Recidivism was greater among younger sociopaths. Eighty-five percent of the 13 reconvicted sociopaths were under age 30 compared to 47 percent of the other 30 (p<.05). A similar trend was seen among the 19 rearrested sociopaths compared to the other

24 (74 percent versus 46 percent), but the difference was not statistically significant.

Six of the 8 sociopaths who had never married were rearrested; 5 were reconvicted. Significantly more of the 19 rearrested sociopaths had never married (32 percent versus 8 percent, p<.05); similarly, among the 13 reconvicted sociopaths, more had never married (38 percent versus 10 percent, p<.05). Never having married and youth were highly correlated, but the sample was too small to control for each variable separately.

The 11 drug-dependent sociopaths under age 30 had the highest recidivism rates: 82 percent rearrested and 64 percent reconvicted.

Discussion

To summarize: one-third of the women were rearrested at least once during the follow-up period; about two-thirds of those rearrested were eventually reconvicted.

The length of parole supervision prior to the index study was negatively correlated with recidivism. No woman who had successfully completed two years of parole before the beginning of the study was rearrested or reconvicted during the follow-up. This may have indicated a therapeutic effect of parole supervision. On the other hand, it may have reflected a selection effect in that those with the highest risk of recidivism may have broken parole earlier. This needs further study, preferably with a consecutive series of criminals interviewed immediately upon assignment to parole supervision.

Young female felons with previous antisocial, delinquent, and criminal behavior (reflected in the diagnosis of sociopathy) were more likely than those without such prior history to become involved in further criminal activities. Drug dependence aggravated this tendency of sociopathic women.

Many of the factors associated with recidivism singly were significantly related to one another. The apparent effect of a single factor on recidivism rates may have resulted from an overlap with other factors. For example, the index crime of robbery was correlated with having never been married, being homosexual, and having been on parole less than one month; each of these variables was in turn associated with a greater risk of recidivism. Consequently, the significance of the association of robbery and recidivism is uncertain until replicated with a different and larger sample. Similarly, sociopathy and homosexuality were each associated with recidivism and with each other. All but one of the homosexuals were also sociopaths, and among the non-homosexual sociopaths recidivism was still increased. Thus, recidivism among sociopaths is not necessarily dependent on homosexuality.

The findings were similar to those obtained in the earlier study of convicted male felons, with one notable difference. Among the men, unlike the women, alcoholism was also associated with increased recidivism rates. The study of male felons was begun in 1959, however, before the widespread increase in drug dependence. It was not possible, therefore, to determine whether the different findings reflected a sex difference or a shift in time in the relative importance of drug dependence and alcoholism.

As was true among the male criminals, there was a definite tendency among female criminals for recidivism rates to fall with age. This "burned-out" phenomenon is well recognized. Whether it represents "greater maturity," "loss of drive," or other factors is not known, but it offers the possibility that ultimately appropriate measures will lead to earlier remissions.

PSYCHIATRIC ILLNESS IN FIRST-DEGREE RELATIVES (15)

Personal Interview Data

The psychiatric diagnoses of the interviewed relatives are presented in Table 32. Eighty-four percent of the relatives received at least one psychiatric diagnosis. A third of the relatives received diagnoses of sociopathy or hysteria. About half received diagnoses of sociopathy, alcoholism, hysteria, or drug dependence. Anxiety neurosis was found in about one in 6. Homosexuality, affective

TABLE 32

PSYCHIATRIC DIAGNOSES BASED ON PERSONAL INTERVIEW ONLY: RELATIVES OF FEMALE FELONS (15)

Psychiatric Diagnosis	Interviewed Men N = 36		Interviewed Women N = 70		Total N = 106	
	f	%	f	%	f	%
Alcoholism						
definite	15		9		24	
questionable	3		4		7	
total	18	50	13	19	31	29
Hysteria						
definite			17		17	
probable			5		5	
total	0	0	22	31	22	21
Sociopathy						
definite	10		7		17	
questionable	1		1		2	
total	11	31	8	11	19	18
Drug Dependence						
total (all definite)	2	6	1	1	3	3
Anxiety Neurosis	7	19	11	16	18	17
Homosexuality						
significant	2		0		2	
casual	1		1		2	
total	3	8	1	1	4	4
Primary Affective Disorder						
bipolar			1		1	
unipolar			2		2	
total	0	0	3	4	3	3
Mental Retardation	0	0	3	4	3	3
Dementia	0	0	1	1	1	1
Schizophrenia						
total (probable)	1	3	0	0	1	1
Undiagnosed Illness						
most like hysteria	0		12		12	
most like sociopathy	1		1		2	
most like depression	0		3		3	
other	1		3		4	
total	2	6	19	27	21	20
Some Psychiatric Illness						
sociopathy or hysteria	11	31	25	36	36	34
alcoholism or drug dependence and not						
sociopathy or hysteria)	8	22	5	7	13	12
other illnesses	9	25	31	44	40	38
total	28	78	61	87	89	84
No Psychiatric Illness	8	22	9	13	17	16

(From Br. J. Psychiatry *122*: 697-703, 1973. Reprinted by permission.)

disorder, and mental retardation were each seen in 3 or 4 percent. There was one case each of schizophrenia and dementia. A fifth of the relatives had an undiagnosed psychiatric illness; over half of these were women with illnesses like hysteria.

Sex Differences. Sociopathy was more common in men than women (31 percent versus 11 percent, p<.05). The same was true for alcoholism (50 percent versus 19 percent, p<.02). Hysteria was seen only among women. An undiagnosed disorder was more common among women (27 percent versus 6 percent, p<.05); this was partly related to the number of cases of questionable hysteria. Conversion symptoms were more frequent in women than in men (61 percent versus 28 percent, p<.01); 50 percent of the relatives reported at least one conversion symptom.

Racial Differences. Hysteria was more frequent among black women than white women (42 percent versus 15 percent, p<.05). Black women also reported conversion symptoms more frequently than white women (74 percent versus 41 percent, p<.02). In contrast, anxiety neurosis was less likely among black men than white men (8 percent versus 42 percent), but the difference was not statistically significant. The high frequency of anxiety neurosis in men was partly due to a marked elevation in white men.

Family History Data

Excluding cases where no information about the relative could be obtained, a total of 676 independent histories for 286 of the relatives were elicited, a mean of 2.4 per relative.

Most relatives appeared to have some psychiatric disorder. Sociopathy or alcoholism was suspected in a third. Schizophrenia, affective disorder, and dementia were suspected in fewer than one percent each.

Record Information

Based on independent records alone, a psychiatric diagnosis could be made in only a fourth of the relatives. Again, sociopathy and alcoholism were the most frequent diagnoses. Evidence of schizophrenia was not present in any of the records.

Overall Diagnoses

Diagnoses based on all information available about interviewed and noninterviewed relatives are presented in Table 33.

TABLE 33
OVERALL PSYCHIATRIC DIAGNOSES BASED ON ALL
AVAILABLE INFORMATION: RELATIVES OF FEMALE
FELONS (15)

Psychiatric Diagnosis	Men Interviewed N = 36		Men Not Interviewed N = 104		Women Interviewed N = 70		Women Not Interviewed N = 78	
	f	%	f	%	f	%	f	%
Alcoholism								
definite	15		5		10		4	
questionable	3		3		4		2	
suspected	4		30		5		9	
total	22	61	38	37	19	27	15	19
Hysteria								
total	0	0	0	0	24	34	0	0
Sociopathy								
definite	11		5		7		0	
questionable	1		5		1		2	
suspected	1		9		0		1	
total	13	36	19	18	8	11	3	4
Drug Dependence								
definite	2		2		1		1	
questionable	1		0		0		0	
suspected	2		1		2		0	
total	5	14	3	3	3	4	1	1
Anxiety Neurosis	7	19	0	0	11	16	0	0
Homosexuality								
significant	2		0	·	0		0	
casual	1		0		1		0	
suspected	1		1		3		0	
total	4	11	1	1	4	6	0	0

111

TABLE 33 (*Continued*)

Psychiatric Diagnosis	Men Interviewed N = 36		Men Not Interviewed N = 104		Women Interviewed N = 70		Women Not Interviewed N = 78	
	f	%	f	%	f	%	f	%
Primary Affective Disorder								
definite	0		0		3		0	
suspected	0		0		1		0	
total	0	0	0	0	4	6	0	0
Mental Retardation	0	0	1	1	3	4	0	0
Dementia	0	0	0	0	1	1	0	0
Schizophrenia								
probable	1		0		0		0	
suspected	0		0		0		1	
total	1	3	0	0	0	0	1	1
No Specific Diagnosis But Ill	2	6	9	9	16	23	20	26
Some Psychiatric Illness								
sociopathy or hysteria	13	36	19	18	27	39	3	4
alcoholism or drug dependence (and not sociopathy or hysteria)	11	31	28	27	10	14	15	19
other illnesses	7	19	11	11	26	37	22	28
total	31	86	58	56	63	90	40	51
No Psychiatric Illness	5	14	46	44	7	10	38	49

(From Br. J. Psychiatry *122*: 697-703, 1973. Reprinted by permission.)

Interviewed Relatives. Of the 106 interviewed relatives, 84 percent received a psychiatric diagnosis on the basis of the interview, and another five percent received a diagnosis on the basis of other information. These additional cases included 3 suspected alcoholics, one suspected sociopath who also appeared to be an alcoholic, and a fifth whose mental hospitalization and imprisonment were revealed only by records and family history. Having received no diagnosis at interview, she was finally considered to have an undiagnosed psychiatric disorder.

Twenty-one interviewed relatives received an overall diagnosis of sociopathy: 19 at interview and one each on the basis of records or family history. One of the latter 2 revealed an acute brain syndrome at the time of interview conducted in hospital and died of associated pericarditis during the same admission. The other reported extensive antisocial behavior but denied police trouble; records revealed a previous felony conviction.

Forty-one interviewed relatives received an overall diagnosis of alcoholism: 31 at interview, one from records, and 9 from family history.

Twenty-four interviewed relatives received an overall diagnosis of hysteria. The diagnosis was made at interview in 22 cases; the other 2 were considered undiagnosed but hysteria was suspected. A definite diagnosis was possible in the latter cases based upon hospital records.

Nine interviewed relatives had some history of homosexuality. Only 4 reported this at interview, however. Only 2 subjects reported repeated and significant homosexuality at interview.

The overall prevalences of anxiety neurosis, affective disorder, schizophrenia, dementia, and mental retardation were essentially the same as those based on interview alone.

Noninterviewed Relatives. Among noninterviewed relatives, overall diagnoses were based on information from family histories and records. Data from the family history were more important in terms of the proportion of relatives who could be classified using it alone.

Of the 182 noninterviewed subjects, 22 received an overall diagnosis of sociopathy. In 10 cases this was suspected from family history alone, in one case the diagnosis was based only on records, and in 11 cases the diagnosis could be made from either records or family history. Thus, the family history alone was sufficient to diagnose sociopathy in 21 of the 22 noninterviewed relatives; in about half, records confirmed the impression.

Alcoholism was the overall diagnosis in 53 noninterviewed relatives. It was based on the family history alone in 39 cases, on records alone in 3 cases, and on both in 11 cases.

There were 4 noninterviewed relatives with the diagnosis of

drug dependence; 3 were based on records and one was based on family history.

No noninterviewed relative received a diagnosis of schizophrenia based on records, but one woman was suspected of suffering from this disorder on the basis of family history. One noninterviewed relative's mental retardation was revealed by I.Q. tests at a mental hospital, and another was considered homosexual on the basis of family history. No noninterviewed relative received the diagnosis of anxiety neurosis, hysteria, affective disorder, or dementia. Twenty-nine noninterviewed relatives who were considered psychiatrically ill were classified as undiagnosed.

All Relatives. Altogether, 67 percent of the relatives received one or more psychiatric diagnoses; 89 percent of the 106 interviewed and 54 percent of the 182 noninterviewed relatives. Sociopathy or hysteria was diagnosed in 22 percent; 38 percent of the interviewed and 12 percent of the noninterviewed relatives. Alcoholism was diagnosed in 33 percent; 57 percent of the interviewed and 19 percent of the noninterviewed relatives. Drug dependence was diagnosed in 4 percent; 8 percent of the interviewed and 2 percent of the noninterviewed relatives.

Other Clinical Data. In addition to diagnosis, certain clinically significant data were obtained from all sources about both interviewed and noninterviewed relatives.

At the time of the study, 48 relatives were dead. Among the 28 dead men, 2 died by suicide (7 percent) and 4 (14 percent) by homicide. None of the 20 dead women committed suicide, but 2 (10 percent) died by homicide.

Thirty-three relatives, or 11 percent, had consulted a psychiatrist; this included 17 relatives, or 6 percent, who had been in a mental hospital at least once. Another 16 relatives, or 6 percent, had been hospitalized in a general hospital for alcoholism or "nervousness," without known psychiatric consultation. Sixteen subjects, or 6 percent, had made unsuccessful suicide attempts. A history of "nervousness" for which medical attention had been sought characterized 103 relatives, or 36 percent. Seventeen subjects, or 6 percent, were said to have had a "nervous breakdown" at some time. Seventy-five subjects, or 26 percent, had been in jail, reform school, or prison.

Discussion

Very high rates of psychopathology, particularly sociopathy, hysteria, alcoholism, and drug dependence, characterized the families of the convicted female felons. The single best source of information was the personal interview, but family history and records added to the overall evaluation. The particularly high rates based upon psychiatric interview warrant further comment.

Using record and family history data, it was possible to compare interviewed and noninterviewed relatives. The records revealed no significant differences between the two groups. A diagnosis of some psychiatric illness based upon family history, however, was more likely in interviewed than noninterviewed relatives (68 percent versus 52 percent, p<.02). The family history-based diagnoses of the two groups were not directly comparable on a subject-to-subject basis, however. The 106 interviewed relatives were the subjects of 349 independent family histories obtained from other interviewed relatives, a mean of 3.3 per subject. In contrast, the 182 noninterviewed relatives were the subjects of 327 such histories, a mean of 1.8 per subject. Psychiatric illness was suspected in 51 percent of the 349 histories about interviewed relatives and in 49 percent of the 327 histories about noninterviewed relatives, essentially similar figures. The figures thus suggest that if more family histories could have been obtained about the noninterviewed subjects, the frequency of suspected diagnoses in the two groups would have been more alike. Thus, the results suggest that the data concerning interviewed subjects are representative of the relatives in general.

The psychiatric disorders in these families were the same as those in the families of male felons, but the overall frequency of psychiatric illness was twice as high in the families of female felons. Since it is unusual for women to be convicted of felonies, they and their families might be expected to show generally greater social and psychological deviance than would be the case for male felons and their families.

The prevalence of anxiety neurosis among the male relatives was higher than expected. Since, however, a much lower proportion of white male relatives than of other categories of relatives was interviewed, the high proportion of white male relatives with anxiety neurosis may have indicated a selection bias in that those interviewed were more likely to cooperate with the interview because of their anxiety neurosis.

Schizophrenia was found in only one interviewed relative. It was diagnosed in only one of the index subjects, but 2 other female felons, with undiagnosed disorders, may have been schizophrenic. The absence of an increased prevalence of schizophrenia in the relatives indicates that disguised or atypical cases of schizophrenia among the index subjects were not missed.

THE ASSOCIATION BETWEEN HYSTERIA AND SOCIOPATHY

The association between hysteria and sociopathy merits further comment because it illustrates how careful follow-up and family studies may identify possible etiological and pathogenetic connections between disorders and thus lead to new research. The findings described earlier—that hysteria and sociopathy cluster in the same families and may be present in the same individual— take on additional significance when combined with the results of other studies.

Lee Robins, in her now classical monograph describing a 30-year follow-up of children seen in a child guidance clinic, reported that 20 of 76 adolescent girls, or 26 percent, referred because of antisocial behavior received a diagnosis of hysteria as adults (86). Forrest reported that antisocial behavior and alcohol or drug abuse are common in patients with hysteria (29). Maddocks found "marked hypochondriacal traits" in a group of untreated sociopaths at follow-up (66). Guze, Woodruff, and Clayton, reporting on a controlled comparison of women with hys-

teria and women with anxiety neurosis, excluding those with con-
comitant diagnoses of sociopathy, noted that women with hysteria
have a more frequent history of personal and familial antisocial
and delinquent behavior (55).

An increased risk of delinquency and sociopathy appears to be
associated with the hyperactive child syndrome (69). Thus, the
results of two studies of the families of hyperactive children are
pertinent (8, 71). In each study, when compared to the parents
of control children, the fathers showed an increased prevalence
of sociopathy and the mothers an increased prevalence of hysteria. Adoptive parents of hyperactive children did not have
similar characteristics (72).

These results strongly support the hypothesis described above
that hysteria and sociopathy are different, though overlapping,
manifestations of the same underlying disorder. The clinical manifestations—whether predominantly those of hysteria or predominantly those of sociopathy—apparently depend primarily on the
sex of the individual.

LONG RANGE FOLLOW-UP

Long-term personal psychiatric and criminal recidivism follow-up
of the women felons and a psychiatric study of their spouses have
not yet been completed.

SIX
Other Studies

Two additional studies, also carried out in this department, complement the work described in the preceding chapters. The first was a study of pretrial psychiatric examinations and the second of a consecutive series of psychiatry clinic patients.

A STUDY OF PRETRIAL PSYCHIATRIC EXAMINATIONS (77)

In the studies of convicted felons described in Chapters 3, 4, and 5, the selection of subjects failed to include individuals who, because of psychiatric evaluation and treatment, were transferred permanently to psychiatric facilities from the courts or prisons. This omission has already been discussed in Chapter 3, where it was pointed out that about 2 percent of the felons were lost in this fashion. A study of prisoners referred to a psychiatric hospital for pretrial psychiatric evaluation afforded an opportunity to correct for this omission, since most of the felons who escaped the selection process described in Chapter 3 were lost before they were imprisoned.

118

This study was carried out on the forensic service of Malcolm Bliss Mental Health Center, a short-term psychiatric hospital in St. Louis, Missouri. The service performs inpatient pretrial evaluations for the courts of the City of St. Louis and several Missouri counties close to St. Louis to determine the presence of psychiatric illness, competency to stand trial, and criminal responsibility. When indicated, the pretrial evaluation may also result in appropriate treatment. Since the facility contains only a medium security unit, pretrial evaluations are not performed for individuals who, in the opinion of the court, present an undue risk of either being physically injurious to others or of escape. Such individuals are hospitalized at another hospital where a maximum security unit is available. During the period of the study, 2 individuals, 4 percent, were so handled.

From August 1973 to March 1974, 50 consecutive prisoners were admitted for pretrial evaluation. They were systematically interviewed, using the interview and diagnostic criteria described in Chapter 3. The index crime and arrest were excluded from consideration for a diagnosis of sociopathy. More than one diagnosis was possible in any individual. Records of previous psychiatric hospitalizations were obtained wherever possible.

Eighty-eight percent of the prisoners were male, 58 percent were white, 56 percent had been married at least once, and over 60 percent of these were currently separated or divorced. The mean age was 31, with a range between 18 and 77. Over 80 percent had not graduated from high school.

Strikingly, 82 percent had been psychiatrically hospitalized prior to the index crime, including 10 of the 11 schizophrenics and all 5 of the subjects with bipolar affective disorder (see below). Half had been in jail prior to the index crime, and another 16 percent had been arrested previously but had not been imprisoned.

The index crime and psychiatric diagnosis for each subject are presented in Table 34; the distribution of diagnoses is summarized in Table 35. Sociopathy (antisocial personality), alcoholism, or drug dependence—with or without other diagnoses—was found in 80 percent. Schizophrenia or bipolar affective disorder was found in 32 percent. Mental retardation and all forms of sexual

TABLE 34
INDEX CRIMES (77)

	N
Larceny	7
Assault with Intent to Kill	6
Burglary	6
Auto Theft	6
Child Molestation	5
Robbery	4
Homicide	3
Drug Related	3
Arson	3
Forgery or Bad Checks	2
Carrying Concealed Weapon	2
Sodomy	2
Assault with Intent to Ravish	1
Manslaughter	1
Bomb Threat	1
Statutory Rape	1
Assaulting a Police Officer	1
	54*

* Four individuals charged with two crimes each.

deviation combined were each seen in 12 percent. Other diagnoses were infrequent.

There were no obvious correlations between a given crime and psychiatric diagnosis. About half of the crimes were against persons; this was true for subjects with schizophrenia or bipolar affective disorder as well as the others.

The very high frequency of previous psychiatric hospitalization (82 percent) strongly suggests that the request for pretrial psychiatric evaluation was primarily based upon this history. The fact that the request for such evaluation usually came from the prisoner's attorney, who, understandably, was looking for information that would help defend his client, is consistent with this conclusion.

The high prevalence of sociopathy, alcoholism, and drug dependence indicates that even in criminals selected because of

TABLE 35
DISTRIBUTION OF DIAGNOSES* (77)

	%
Sociopathy	50
Alcoholism	48
Drug Dependence	26
Schizophrenia	22
Mental Retardation	12
Sexual Deviation (Pedophilia or Homosexuality)	12
Bipolar Affective Disorder	10
Secondary Depression	6
Organic Brain Syndrome	4
Hysteria (Briquet's Syndrome)	2
Epilepsy	2
Undiagnosed Psychiatric Illness	6

* More than one diagnosis was possible for each subject.

suspected psychiatric illness, these disorders are characteristically present, demonstrating again the important role they play in criminality. Since the sample was selected because of suspected psychiatric illness, it is not surprising that nearly a third of the prisoners received diagnoses of either schizophrenia or bipolar affective disorder. This is particularly to be expected when the suspicion of psychiatric illness is based largely upon a history of previous psychiatric hospitalization. Eight of the 16 subjects (50 percent) with either schizophrenia or bipolar affective disorder received additional diagnoses of alcoholism (7 cases) or drug dependence (one case), and 11 (70 percent) received diagnoses of sociopathy, alcoholism, or drug dependence. Schizophrenia or bipolar affective disorder uncomplicated by these three conditions appear, therefore, to be infrequent among criminals, even including those suspected of psychiatric illness.

To summarize: the studies described in Chapters 4 and 5 indicated that schizophrenia or primary affective disorder occurred in about 2 percent of convicted felons. Since about 2 percent of the felons were missed because of presumed psychiatric difficulty, as already discussed, and only a third of the criminals identified because psychiatric illness was suspected received diagnoses of schizophrenia or primary affective disorder, the previous conclusions were confirmed: these disorders are infrequent in apprehended or convicted felons. Finally, even the few cases of schizophrenia and primary affective disorder were often complicated by alcoholism or drug dependence.

PSYCHIATRY CLINIC PATIENTS (56)

Having approached the question, "What kinds of psychiatric disorders are associated with criminality?" first by studying convicted criminals, it seemed appropriate to study psychiatric patients, asking the same question.

Five hundred patients were selected, between July 1, 1967 and October 31, 1969, as a representative cross section of our psychiatry clinic population, for systematic long-term, clinical, follow-up, and family studies. The data to be described here were obtained from these patients at the original interview. The research interview and diagnostic criteria were slightly modified from those described in Chapter 3 (23, 103) but essentially covered the same material and identified the same disorders. As noted in Chapter 3, the interview included a section dealing with police trouble and imprisonment. The interview records were restudied to determine which patients had ever been convicted of a felony.

A history of at least one felony conviction was given by 22 patients, for a total of 26 convictions. This represented 4 percent of the entire sample, 10 percent of the men and one percent of the women. The sex difference is statistically significant ($p<.01$), but no accompanying significant differences between the races controlled for sex were noted.

Crimes for which the patients had been convicted, in order of frequency, were burglary (6 cases), robbery (5 cases), exhibitionism (4 cases), larceny (3 cases), forgery and shoplifting (2 cases each), and attempted rape, auto theft, illegal possession of a weapon, child molestation (one case each).

Sexual deviation led directly to crime in 5 patients: 4 cases of exhibitionism and one case of child molestation. Further, one case of larceny involved stealing women's clothes as an indirect manifestation of sexual deviation (fetishism). Therefore, 6 of the 22 patients (all men) were convicted because of behavior directly resulting from sexual deviation. In 5 of these men, no other psychiatric diagnosis was made; one man was an alcoholic.

relyon

Of the remaining 16 patients, 14 were either sociopaths, alcoholics, or drug dependent. Sociopathy was present in 13 of these cases, alcoholism in 8, and drug dependence in 3.

Anxiety neurosis was diagnosed in one patient: a 34-year-old black woman who had been convicted of shoplifting six years earlier. The remaining patient was a 17-year-old black teenager with a history of delinquent and criminal behavior, who, however, just failed to meet the criteria for a diagnosis of sociopathy; he was considered undiagnosed.

A felony conviction was thus reported by 37 percent of the 35 sociopaths, 13 percent of 70 alcoholics, 23 percent of the 13 drug-dependent individuals, 2 percent of the 62 anxiety neurotics, and one percent of the more than 100 undiagnosed patients in the entire sample of 500. One of the 16 mentally retarded patients was also a sociopath, an alcoholic, and had been convicted of a felony. None of the other 15 with mental retardation had such a history.

Most importantly, none of the more than 200 patients with either a schizophrenic or primary affective disorder reported a felony conviction.

To summarize: the results from a study of psychiatric patients were consistent with those from the studies of apprehended or convicted felons. Sociopathy, alcoholism, and drug dependence are the principal psychiatric disorders associated with serious crime. Aside from sexual deviation leading directly or indirectly to arrest and conviction, other psychiatric disorders are infrequently associated with serious crime.

SEVEN

Conclusions and Discussion

CRIME AND PSYCHIATRIC DISORDERS

Recapitulation of Diagnostic Findings

The results of all phases of the study are consistent. Sociopathy, alcoholism, and drug dependence are the psychiatric disorders characteristically associated with serious crime. Schizophrenia, primary affective disorders, anxiety neurosis, obsessional neurosis, phobic neurosis, and brain syndromes are not. Sexual deviations, defined as illegal *per se,* are not, in the absence of accompanying sociopathy, alcoholism, and drug dependence, associated with other serious crime.

While hysteria (Briquet's Syndrome) is frequent among female felons, felony conviction is not common among hysterics. In addition, since serious crime is relatively infrequent among women, the association between hysteria and serious crime is of restricted general importance.

The special features of these studies—systematic psychiatrically unbiased selection of both male and female criminals, use of a standardized research interview, application of explicit diagnostic criteria based upon independent follow-up and family studies, repeated follow-up based on multiple records and personal interviews, and systematic study of first-degree relatives and spouses—contribute to the confidence that can be placed in the results.

A further comment is indicated concerning the possible association between illnesses such as schizophrenia, primary affective disorders, or brain syndromes and criminal behavior. Many experienced psychiatrists have seen occasional patients with these illnesses who have also committed some illegal act. Often the criminal act apparently arose directly from the illness, that is, in response to delusions or hallucinations. Such clinical observations appear to contradict the findings of this investigation. Actually there is no contradiction. While such illness-related crimes occur, they are infrequent and therefore contribute little to the overall association between crime and psychiatric illness.

Schizophrenia, primary affective disorders, or brain syndromes may play more significant roles in certain types of crime, and studies of special categories of crime might result in different findings. Noteworthy in this regard is the frequency of primary depressions reported in individuals involved in homicide followed by suicide. West found that in Great Britain about a quarter of homicides are followed by suicide whereas in the United States the figure is less than 10 percent (98). Thus, in Great Britain primary affective disorders play a more important role in homicides than they do in the United States. Further, since homicide is, fortunately, relatively infrequent compared to other felonies, studies of felonies in general are not likely to uncover a strong association between general criminality and primary affective illnesses.

In short, it is unlikely that further studies of unselected felons will result in different findings. The relative importance of alcoholism or drug dependence may vary from community to community and from time to time, but it is not likely that the relative frequency of schizophrenia or primary affective disorder would prove different.

Other Studies

It may be useful at this point to review the findings from other studies and compare them with the results of the present investigation. The following representative reports in English were all available before the present investigation was begun.

In 1918, Glueck reported on the prevalence of psychiatric illness in 608 of 683 consecutive male admissions to Sing Sing Prison from August 1, 1916 to April 30, 1917 (34). Without providing diagnostic criteria, he reported that 59 percent of his men were psychiatrically ill: 12 percent suffered from some form of psychosis (half were found to have schizophrenia), 28 percent were mentally defective, and 19 percent were psychopaths. He did not discuss alcoholism, neuroses or neurotic symptoms, and, while he discussed the types of crimes committed by the various categories of criminals, there was no discussion of prognosis or follow-up.

In 1937, Thompson reported on the presence of psychiatric illness in a group of 1,380 criminals (95). He studied all the recidivists seen in a court of general sessions in 1935. He found that 0.6 percent of the criminals were psychotic, 2.6 percent were mentally defective, and 5.6 percent were psychopaths. No other diagnoses were made, no diagnostic criteria were presented, and no follow-up was reported.

In 1947, Bromberg and Thompson reported on psychiatric observations of nearly 10,000 convicted criminals seen in the psychiatry clinic of the court of general sessions in New York City (7). The intensity of the examinations varied from a special screening for all to a more detailed individual study of some of the prisoners. Without discussing diagnostic criteria except in very general terms, they found the following percentages of psychiatric illness: mental deficiency, 2.4 percent; psychoses, 1.5 percent; psychopathy, 6.9 percent; and psychoneurosis, 6.9 percent. The remainder were regarded as psychiatrically normal, but an attempt was made to categorize them by personality types. Alcoholism was not discussed. There was no discussion of differences in crimes or prognosis based upon the presence or absence of psychiatric disorder.

In 1940, Selling reported on 500 consecutive traffic offenders referred by the judge for psychiatric evaluation (89). This was a highly selected group without indication as to how they were selected (that is, the judge's criteria were not presented), nor is it known what fraction of the total group of traffic offenders is represented by the sample. The following figures were presented: I.Q. less than 70, 36 percent; alcoholism, 35.8 percent; chronic alcoholism, 15.2 percent; personality disorders and psychoneuroses, 2.2 percent; and psychoses, 2.2 percent. No follow-up data were presented.

Oltman and Friedman, in 1941, reported their findings from a study of 100 consecutive criminals committed to a psychiatric hospital for observation (74). The criteria for commitment are not clear. They found the following: 26 percent of the criminals were psychotic, 16 percent were mentally defective, 14 percent were psychopaths, 3 percent were psychoneurotic, and the rest were "without psychosis" and presumably without any of the other psychiatric disorders. Diagnostic criteria were not presented though the psychotic group was further broken down into 9 cases of dementia praecox, 8 cases of CNS syphilis, 3 cases of manic-depressive disease, 2 cases of alcoholic psychosis, and 2 cases of "psychosis with psychopathic personality." The mentally defective group included one case of "mental deficiency with psychosis." There was no follow-up, and no data relating illness to prognosis were presented. Except for the cases of alcoholic psychosis, alcoholism was not discussed.

In 1942, Banay (4) reported on the prevalence of alcoholism among Sing Sing prisoners. His data are difficult to interpret because he attempted to distinguish "alcoholic criminals from the criminals who are alcoholic," referring in the latter group to alcoholism that did not seem to play a causal role in the criminal careers of his subjects. Nevertheless, it is clear that about half of his subjects received a diagnosis of some sort of alcoholism. Diagnostic criteria were not given. Other psychiatric disorders were not studied, and no follow-up was included.

In 1946, Silverman reported a study of 500 consecutive psychotic criminals admitted to the Springfield Medical Center for federal prisoners (90). Without discussing diagnostic criteria, he compared his subjects with nonpsychotic criminals, using federal prison statistics for the latter. He found few differences in the family, personal, and social backgrounds, or types of crimes between the two groups. There was no follow-up.

Wolfgang, in 1958, published his major study on criminal homicide (102), emphasizing, among many other things, the high frequency with which alcohol use was associated with homicide. He did not study alcoholism, as such, nor did he study other psychiatric diagnoses. There was no follow-up.

After the first paper describing the present investigation was published (49), a number of researchers reported high frequencies of alcoholism among various groups of criminals. Unfortunately, diagnostic criteria were not usually described, and the presence of other psychiatric disorders was generally not studied. Psychiatric follow-up was not part of the research design, and no study of relatives was included.

In 1963, Cramer and Blacker (19) reported that 80 percent of white female inmates of the Massachusetts Correctional Institute in Framingham, Massachusetts were problem drinkers.

Gillies, in 1965, reported psychiatric findings in 66 persons accused of murder in the Glasgow area of Scotland (33). The author states that "it has been increasingly the practice . . . to obtain psychiatric opinion on the mental state of all persons accused of murder," implying that his subjects were not selected because of manifest psychiatric disturbances. He found that "the causal factors in this series . . . fell into three large classes: drunkenness, psychopathy and schizophrenia." Fifteen percent of the subjects were schizophrenic, 27 percent were psycopaths, and 55 percent "were affected by alcohol at the time of the offenses." The report does not provide information to determine how many of the latter were chronic alcoholics.

In 1966, in a study of 50 recently discharged male prisoners "who called at the office of the Royal London Discharged Prisoners Aid Society for help and advice," Maule and Cooper (68), found that "no fewer than . . . 56 percent . . . were judged to have drinking problems."

Gibbens and Silberman (32), in 1970, reported a study "of 404 prisoners and ex-prisoners from three . . . London prisons . . . 40 percent were found to be excessive drinkers, although drunken offenders with very short sentences were excluded."

In 1971, Edwards, Hensman, and Peto (22) reviewed the general relationship between alcohol and crime and identified methodologic problems relevant to surveys of the prevalence of alcoholism in prison populations. Their data suggest that problem drinking or alcoholism are frequent in such populations.

In 1972, in a paper entitled *Drugs and Crime*, Tinklenberg summarized several of the above studies as well as others and presented new data of his own. He concluded that the use of alcohol and problem drinking are frequently associated with serious crimes (96).

In 1973, Nicol *et al.* (73) studied the relationship of alcoholism to violent behavior resulting in long-term imprisonment. They reported high rates of alcoholism in all prisoners, with the highest rates associated with histories of greater violence.

Tupin, Mahar, and Smith (97), in 1973, reported a study of 50 male murderers incarcerated at California Medical Facility, the psychiatric institution for the California Department of Corrections. They found that only 12 percent of these highly selected individuals were considered schizophrenic or psychotic. Most were considered to have personality disorders.

Studies of criminality in psychiatric patients have been much less frequent than studies of psychiatric disorders among criminals.

In a report based on the arrest record of 5,354 male ex-patients released from the New York State Mental Hospital during the period 1946-48, Brill and Malzberg (6) concluded that "patients with no record of crime or arrest have a strikingly low rate of arrest after release," and "patients who have a prior record of arrest have a rate of rearrest which compares favorably with figures available for persons in the general population who have an arrest record." Unfortunately, no diagnostic breakdown is provided for the former patients so that it is not possible to estimate the relative risk of arrest in different psychiatric conditions.

129

A lower arrest rate for former psychiatric inpatients than for the general population was reported by Ashley (3), Pollock (79), and Cohen and Freeman (18).

In contrast, from a study of patients discharged from Maryland state psychiatric hospitals during fiscal years 1947 and 1957, Rappeport reported (82, 83) that "women with a history of psychiatric hospitalization are more likely to be arrested for aggressive assault than are women in the general population" and that men had "a significantly higher arrest rate" for robbery than did the general population. Unfortunately, though some diagnostic data are provided, diagnostic criteria are not described, and it is not possible to estimate satisfactorily from the data presented the role of sociopathy and alcoholism in the increased arrest rates.

In an extensive review of the Continental European literature, particularly German, Dutch, and Scandinavian publications describing psychiatric studies of criminals and studies of crime in psychiatric patients, Wiersma (100) attempted to assess the relationship between schizophrenia and crime and concluded that "among schizophrenics, criminals are probably not more frequent than among so-called normal subjects."

Similarly, in a report from West Germany (57), Häfner and Böker concluded that "crimes of violence committed by mentally ill and mentally retarded are quantitatively proportional to the number of crimes of violence committed by the total population." By mentally ill, the authors were referring specifically to schizophrenia and affective psychosis.

Overall, the other studies may be summarized as follows. Psychosis, schizophrenia, primary affective disorders, and the various neurotic disorders are seen in only a minority of identified criminals. There is no complete agreement as to whether any of these conditions is more common among criminals than the general population, but it is clear that these disorders carry only a *slightly* increased risk of criminality *if any at all*. Though not always considered, when studied, alcoholism and sociopathy are found to be very common among criminals. Further, the role of drug dependence in criminality has only recently been systematically evaluated (21, 96). Finally, even in studies of criminals suspected of serious psychiatric illness, most subjects are not schizophrenic or psychotic.

SOCIAL, FAMILIAL, AND PERSONAL BACKGROUND OF CRIMINALS

It is clear that convicted felons characteristically come from severely disordered families and social backgrounds. Poverty; homes broken by parental death, desertion, divorce, and separation; parental criminality and alcoholism; and restricted opportunity are nearly always present.

From an early age, the felon-to-be reveals the transmission of the social and familial disorder. Repeated delinquent and antisocial behavior precede serious crime in the great majority. Alcohol and drug abuse are very frequent; they typically also begin early and aggravate the antisocial tendencies.

Repeated social and interpersonal difficulties resulting in limited formal education, impaired ability to hold a job for extended periods and thus achieve a position of greater responsibility and reward, and poor marital adjustment leading to separation and divorce converge to limit the individual's capacity for satisfactory social adjustment. Even among those felons who apparently stop committing serious crimes, long-term achievement is modest. Without education or training, significant job experience, stable marriage, or support from close relatives, overcoming the handicaps of repeated delinquency and crime is very difficult for most former felons.

Instead, they all too often set the stage for repeating the pattern with their own children. Since they frequently marry men or women from similar backgrounds and with similar personal histories, their children often carry a double handicap as they develop and mature in what will be, at best, a minimally satisfactory environment.

Such children, at high risk for careers in delinquency and

crime, are not difficult to identify. The Gluecks (35) and L. Robins (86), among others, have shown that these children can be recognized early.

Data from our study of first-degree relatives of convicted male felons indicate the predictive value of early antisocial behavior, particularly in school (52). Table 36 shows the effect of school delinquency on other forms of maladjustment and on criminality. It is nearly always associated with increased rates for these con-

TABLE 36

DELINQUENCY, SOCIAL MALADJUSTMENT, AND CRIME (52)
(INTERVIEWED FIRST-DEGREE RELATIVES)
THE ROLE OF SCHOOL DELINQUENCY

	Males		Females	
	With History of School Delinquency* (N=50) %	Without History of School Delinquency (N=52) %	With History of School Delinquency* (N=34) %	Without History of School Delinquency (N=124) %
History of Excessive Fighting*	52 †	12	15 †	0
Poor Job History in Those	(N=45)	(N=49)	(N=24)	(N=93)
Who Had Worked*	24 ‡	8	8	2
History of Divorce or Separation of Those	(N=38)	(N=46)	(N=30)	(N=111)
Ever Married	26	26	33	37
History of Military Service Difficulties	(N=19)	(N=17)		
of Those in Service	32	24		
History of Traffic Arrests	68 ‡	44	15	6
History of Nontraffic Arrests	52 ‡	31	18 ‡	6
History of Being Jailed	36	27	12 ‡	1
History of Felony Conviction	18 ‡	4	0	1

* Includes definite and questionable cases in each category.
† Difference between the two values significant at p<.01 level.
‡ Difference between the two values significant at p<.05 level.
(From Dis. Nerv. Syst. 29: 238-243, 1968. Reprinted by permission.)

ditions. In view of the generally pessimistic picture deriving from any review of the results of current prison and parole practices, it would appear that the best hope for the future might lie in the direction of early recognition and vigorous efforts at prevention. But here much more research is needed before preventive measures will have a firm base of knowledge.

The powerful effect of social, economic, and familial circumstances in the genesis of delinquency and crime is by now universally recognized. Vigorous and extensive efforts to eliminate poverty and racism, and their pernicious consequences, are clearly called for—and not only to reduce delinquency and crime. At the same time, however, it must be appreciated that not all criminals have been exposed to poverty or racism and, most important, many men and women burdened by poverty and racism do not become delinquents or criminals (52). Tables 37-39 indicate that many first-degree relatives of convicted male felons, exposed to the same adverse social and family circumstances, are free of delinquency and criminality. Research is indicated to identify, define, and clarify factors responsible for this.

WHITE COLLAR CRIME

Crimes such as income tax evasion, violation of antitrust laws, fraudulent stock schemes, other business frauds, false advertising, and bribery of government officials—so-called white collar crimes (31)—probably are associated with different patterns of psychopathology. There are no systematic psychiatric studies of individuals convicted of such crimes, but what is known about the backgrounds of these persons—business executives and entrepreneurs—suggests that serious psychiatric disorders, such as schizophrenia, affective disorders, sociopathy, alcoholism, and drug dependence, are not present to an increased degree. In fact, it is likely that these conditions are quite infrequent among such individuals.

While the total impact of such criminal activity on the community may be very great, conviction for white collar crime is *com-*

TABLE 37

DELINQUENCY, SOCIAL MALADJUSTMENT, AND CRIME (52)
(INTERVIEWED FIRST-DEGREE RELATIVES)
BY SEX AND RACE

	White Men (N= 71) %	Black Men (N= 31) %	Total Men (N= 102) %	White Women (N= 112) %	Black Women (N= 46) %	Total Women (N= 158) %	Total (N= 260) %
History of School Delinquency							
Definite:	39	52	44	12	17	14	25
Questionable:	7	3	6	7	9	8	7
Total:	46	55	50	19	26	22	32
History of Excessive Fighting							
Definite	23	35	27	3	2	3	12
Questionable:	6	3	5	0	2	1	2
Total:	29	38	32	3	4	4	14
Poor Job History in Those Who Had Worked	(N= 66)	(N= 28)	(N= 94)	(N= 93)	(N= 34)	(N= 117)	(N= 211)
Definite:	5	21	10	1	0	1	5
Questionable:	5	11	7	3	0	2	5
Total:	10	32	17	4	0	3	10
History of Divorce or Separation of Those Ever Married	(N= 58)	(N= 26)	(N= 84)	(N= 103)	(N= 38)	(N= 141)	(N= 225)
	24	31	26	40	29	37	33
History of Military Service Difficulties of Those in Service	(N= 30)	(N= 6)	(N= 36)				
Not Leading to Court Martial	23	0	19				
Court Martial & Honorable Discharge	7	0	6				
Court Martial & Nonhonorable Discharge	3	0	3				
Total	33	0	28				
History of Traffic Arrests	58	55	57	11	2	8	27
History of Nontraffic Arrests	34	58	41	6	13	8	21
History of Being Jailed	24	48	31	4	0	3	14
History of Felony Conviction	4	26	11	0	2	1	5

(From Dis. Nerv. Syst. 29: 238-243, 1968. Reprinted by permission.)

TABLE 38

DELINQUENCY, SOCIAL MALADJUSTMENT, AND CRIME (52)
(INTERVIEWED FIRST-DEGREE RELATIVES)
BY CATEGORY OF RELATIVE

	Father (N=31) %	Brother (N=69) %	Son (N=2) %	Mother (N=58) %	Sister (N=94) %	Daughter (N=6) %
History of School Delinquency*	39	54	100	7	32	0
History of Excessive Fighting*	23	35	50	3	3	0
Poor Job History in Those Who Had Worked*	(N=31) 10	(N=61) 20	(N=2) 0	(N=42) 2	(N=72) 3	(N=1) 0
History of Divorce or Separation of Those Ever Married	(N=31) 32	(N=51) 24	(N=2) 0	(N=58) 43	(N=78) 33	(N=5) 0
History of Military Service Difficulties of Those in Service	(N=8) 25	(N=27) 30	(N=2) 0			
History of Traffic Arrests	52	60	0	7	10	0
History of Non-traffic Arrests	45	41	0	7	5	0
History of Being Jailed	23	36	0	3	3	0
History of Felony Conviction	0	16	0	2	0	0

* Includes definite and questionable cases in each category.

(From Dis. Nerv. Syst. 29: 238-243, 1968. Reprinted by permission.)

paratively rare. White collar crimes therefore are not likely to have a striking influence in any study of apprehended criminals.

But questions remain. Is a smaller proportion of white collar crimes apprehended and punished than crimes on the FBI Index? Is the harm to the community greater from white collar crimes than from Index crimes? It is obvious that views on these matters will vary widely, and satisfactory answers are not yet available.

TABLE 39

CRIME HISTORY: BY RACE AND CATEGORY OF RELATIVE (52)
(NONINTERVIEWED MALE RELATIVES)

	White Men (N=108) %	Black Men (N=50) %	Fathers (N=63) %	Brothers (N=92) %	Sons (N=3) %	Total Men (N=158) %
History of Arrests	19	28	14	25	67	22
History of Being Jailed	19	26	13	24	67	21
History of Felony Conviction	16	24	10	23	33	18

(From Dis. Nerv. Syst. *29:* 238-243, 1968. Reprinted by permission.)

But these questions deal with important issues concerning the definition and classification of crime. Bribery of public officials, antitrust violations, and violations of safety and antipollution laws may do more harm to many more people than robbery, burglary, larceny, and auto theft put together. The former crimes, even if they are numerically less frequent, perhaps should receive more attention and concern, because a single violation may affect thousands or millions of people.

IMPLICATIONS FOR PENOLOGY AND THE MANAGEMENT OF CRIMINALS

One of the hopes motivating studies such as those reported here is that something will be learned to point the way to a more satisfactory response to criminality. If, for example, a sizeable proportion of convicted felons were found to be suffering from a disorder for which effective treatment is possible in many cases, such treatment could be initiated, for example, phenothiazines for schizophrenia, or antidepressants, ECT, or lithium for primary affective disorders.

But the findings indicate that few felons suffer from these disorders. The great majority are sociopaths, alcoholics, or drug dependent. And, unfortunately, available treatments for these conditions are still not dependable in most cases. So, while efforts to treat these disorders are appropriate, it is difficult to be persuaded that current psychiatric treatment is likely to be very effective. But the data may indicate a way to reduce criminal recidivism. The striking reduction in recidivism associated with increasing age suggests that this variable might be used to plan a more effective program of imprisonment and rehabilitation of convicted criminals. Individuals convicted of serious crime, or those with a history of previous felony convictions, could be imprisoned until they reach an age at which the risk of recidivism is markedly reduced, which, on the basis of the studies reported here, is approximately age 40. By combining age and extent of prior criminality, it appears possible to identify groups of convicted felons with strikingly different risks of recidivism. It was seen in Chapter 3 that the risk of reconviction of a felony was 60 percent in men under age 40 who were also flat-timers compared to six percent in men 40 or older who were parolees—a tenfold difference. Flat-timers differed from parolees primarily in having had one or more previous convictions for a felony or, in some cases, from having been convicted of a very serious crime, such as murder or rape.

It is frequently asserted that criminal recidivism is not high among released murderers. If true, the observation may reflect a general tendency for murderers to receive longer sentences and so not be returned to society until they approach or reach well into middle age.

Imprisonment until middle age, at least for recidivist criminals, should result in a major reduction in recidivism after discharge from prison. This course of action, if adopted, would be justified by the pessimism surrounding current rehabilitation practices and accomplishments. Unless more effective procedures are developed for rehabilitating convicted criminals, it may offer the only hope of reducing this important component of serious crimes. Well over two-thirds of all persons arrested for felonies are "repeaters" (61).

N. Morris, however, has argued against imprisonment based

upon a prediction of future criminality (70). He notes that such prediction will be incorrect in many cases. He points out therefore that "incarceration based on predicted dangerousness is unjust . . . because of fundamental views of human dignity. . . . Fairness and justice in the individual case, not a generalized costbenefit utilitarian weighing, dictate the choice." This view needs further study and consideration. Some of the same arguments might be applied against any incarceration, since some individuals will not commit further crimes even without imprisonment. Important philosophical and ethical issues are involved and need additional discussion and clarification before implementing a policy of prolonged imprisonment designed to prevent future crime rather than to punish past crime. Nevertheless, the data indicate that such prolonged imprisonment for recidivist criminals offers a strong likelihood of reducing criminal recidivism.

COMPETENCY TO STAND TRIAL AND CRIMINAL RESPONSIBILITY IN THE INSANITY DEFENSE

The psychiatric findings in these studies bear on issues concerning competency to stand trial and criminal responsibility in the insanity defense. *Competency* refers to "a mental capacity to participate effectively in the defense of a criminal charge," and *responsibility* refers to "that capacity or incapacity of mind which renders an offender liable or not liable to criminal condemnation for his act . . ." (67).

There exist in American jurisdictions three rules relating to responsibility (67). The first and oldest is the M'Naghten Rule adopted in England in 1843. It holds that a person is not liable to conviction as a criminal if "at the time of the committing of the act, the party accused was laboring under such a defect of reason, from disease of the mind, as not to know the nature and quality of the act he was doing; or, if he did know it, that he did not know he was doing what was wrong." The second is the Durham Rule, promulgated in 1954 in the District of Columbia. It holds that "an accused is not criminally responsible if his unlawful act was the product of mental disease or defect." The third rule is that of the American Law Institute Model Penal Code. It proposes that "(1) A person is not responsible for criminal conduct if at the time of such conduct as the result of mental disease or defect he lacks substantial capacity even to appreciate the criminality of his conduct or to conform his conduct to the requirements of the law. (2) The terms 'mental disease or defect' do not include an abnormality manifested by repeated criminal or otherwise antisocial conduct."

The rule concerning competency to stand trial is generally stated as follows (67): "an accused may not be tried on a criminal charge if at the time of the proceedings against him his mental condition is such that he cannot appreciate the nature of the proceedings and participate intelligently in his defense." The rule concerning competency "is a rule of longstanding in Anglo-American criminal law. It has been assumed to be a rule of constitutional stature and therefore beyond the reach of legislative or judicial change, short of constitutional amendment. . . ." (Quotations from *Mental Disability and The Criminal Law*, copyright 1970 by the American Bar Foundation. Reprinted by permission.)

It is interesting that the responsibility rules have been a source of great controversy and extensive analysis (36) whereas there has been relatively little discussion of competency despite the fact that the issue of responsibility is raised very infrequently in American courts, probably not more often than in one percent of felony cases, while questions of competency to stand trial are much more frequent, and the two issues are closely intertwined as a practical matter even though legally distinct (67).

Few American courts have been willing to accept sociopathy, alcoholism, or drug dependence as indications of mental disorders within the definition of diminished responsibility for the insanity defense. Further, these conditions usually do not interfere with competency to stand trial. Thus, questions of competency and responsibility arise in only a small percentage of felony cases.

Many would argue, on theoretical grounds, that sociopathy, alcoholism, or drug dependence should be considered psychiatric disorders qualifying for the diminished responsibility defense. But, until psychiatric treatment for these conditions is consistently and predictably effective, it could be argued that there is no advantage, and perhaps some disadvantage, to handling such individuals in a hospital for the criminally insane rather than in a penitentiary.

THE NATURE OF SOCIOPATHY

There are two main views about sociopathy. One holds that it is a sociological state caused by poverty, racism, disrupted family life, inadequate housing, and limited education. The other holds that it is a personality pattern caused by constitutional and individual developmental factors. These views are obviously not incompatible and may, on the contrary, be complementary.

As noted earlier, the role of social and familial factors in the genesis of sociopathy is generally recognized. On the other hand, the role of constitutional or biological factors is still debated. Everyone would agree that Cathy Ames in *East of Eden* is a sociopath, but not everyone would agree with John Steinbeck's discussion of sociopathy (93).

> I believe there are monsters born in the world to human parents. Some you can see, misshapen and horrible, with huge heads or tiny bodies; some are born with no arms, no legs, some with three arms, some with tails or mouths in odd places. They are accidents and no one's fault, as used to be thought. Once they were considered the visible punishments for concealed sins.
>
> And just as there are physical monsters, can there not be mental or psychic monsters born? The face and body may be perfect, but if a twisted gene or a malformed egg can produce physical monsters, may not the same process produce a malformed soul?
>
> Monsters are variations from the accepted normal to a greater or a less degree. As a child may be born without an arm, so one may be born without kindness or the potential of conscience. A man who loses his arms in an accident has a great struggle to adjust himself

to the lack, but one born without arms suffers only from people who find him strange. Having never had arms, he cannot miss them. Sometimes when we are little we imagine how it would be to have wings, but there is no reason to suppose it is the same feeling birds have. No, to a monster the norm must seem monstrous, since everyone is normal to himself. To the inner monster it must be even more obscure, since he has no visible thing to compare with others. To a man born without conscience, a soul-stricken man must seem ridiculous. To a criminal, honesty is foolish. You must not forget that a monster is only a variation, and that to a monster the norm is monstrous.

It is my belief that Cathy Ames was born with the tendencies, or lack of them, which drove and forced her all of her life. Some balance wheel was misweighted, some gear out of ratio. She was not like other people, never was from birth. And just as a cripple may learn to utilize his lack so that he becomes more effective in a limited field than the uncrippled, so did Cathy, using her difference, make a painful and bewildering stir in her world.

(Quotations from *East of Eden,* copyright 1952 by John Steinbeck. Reprinted by permission of the Viking Press, Inc.)

Cleckley, in his classic *Mask of Sanity* (11), shares Steinbeck's view of sociopathy as a disorder comparable to schizophrenia in its profound disturbance of the patient's personality and life.

Evidence of a constitutional basis for sociopathy comes from several sources. There are two studies, one from Denmark (88) and one from the United States (20), indicating that children of sociopaths separated from their biological parents early in life and raised by unrelated adoptive parents continue to show increased rates of sociopathy and criminality. There are two additional studies (10, 91), both European, indicating significantly higher concordance rates for sociopathy in monozygotic twins than in same-sexed dizygotic twins. These studies suggest some hereditary predisposition to sociopathy.

The possible association between the XYY karyotype and violent crime (59), the apparently increased prevalence of nonspecifically disordered electroencephalograms in sociopaths (2), and the association between the hyperactive child syndrome, considered by many to be a manifestation of brain dysfunction or im-

141

paired maturation (87), and sociopathy (8, 69, 71, 72) lend support to the view that *at least some cases* of sociopathy may arise from "abnormal" or "altered" brain function. The nature of the brain disturbance is as yet unknown.

A tentative formulation at this time might be as follows. Sociopathy is a heterogeneous condition. It is seen much more frequently in grossly disturbed families and under adverse socioeconomic circumstances. Hereditary predisposition and abnormal brain function may characterize some cases. The earliest manifestations of the disorder might take the form of a hyperactive child syndrome, *though only some of these children become sociopaths.* Because of many genotype-environment correlations and interactions (65), referring to nonrandom environments associated with different genotypes, it is not yet possible to unravel the tangled skein of evidence concerning heredity and environment in sociopathy, but it is difficult to ignore completely the indications of a biological contribution to its etiology.

ALCOHOLISM, DRUG DEPENDENCE, AND CRIME

That alcoholism and drug dependence complicate and aggravate sociopathy and criminality is indicated by the findings described in the earlier chapters. Their role in criminal recidivism has been studied systematically only to a limited extent (21, 39, 43, 47), but their frequent association with crime and delinquency is now recognized (see earlier literature review).

Data from the study of first-degree male relatives of convicted male felons (51, 52), summarized in Tables 40 and 41, provide additional evidence that alcoholism is associated with delinquency, social maladjustment, and crime. It is evident that alcoholism and delinquency (as manifested by school delinquency) have independent effects that may summate. Thus, 25 percent of male relatives with a history of school delinquency *and* alcoholism were convicted of a felony in contrast to the absence of felony convictions in male relatives without a history of school delinquency *or* alcoholism. Relatives with *either* school delin-

TABLE 40

DELINQUENCY, SOCIAL MALADJUSTMENT, AND CRIME (52)
(INTERVIEWED FIRST-DEGREE RELATIVES)
SCHOOL DELINQUENCY AND ALCOHOLISM (MALES ONLY)

	History of School Delinquency[*]		No History of School Delinquency	
	Alcoholics[*] (N=20) %	Nonalcoholics (N=30) %	Alcoholics[*] (N=14) %	Nonalcoholics (N=38) %
History of Excessive Fighting[*a]	70 ‡	40	29 ‡	5
Poor Job History in Those Who Had Worked[*a]	(N=20) 50 †	(N=25) 4	(N=14) 14	(N=35) 6
History of Divorce or Separation of Those Ever Married	(N=17) 35	(N=21) 19	(N=14) 29	(N=32) 25
History of Military Service Difficulties of Those in Service[b]	(N=8) 63 ‡	(N=11) 9	(N=3) 33	(N=14) 21
History of Traffic Arrests[a]	90 ‡	53	43	45
History of Non-traffic Arrests[a]	75 ‡	37	71 †	16
History of Being Jailed[a]	60 ‡	20	57 ‡	16
History of Felony Conviction[b]	25	13	14 ‡	0

[*] Includes definite and questionable cases in each category.
† Difference between the two values significant at p<.01 level.
‡ Difference between the two values significant at p<.05 level.
[a] Difference between alcoholics with history of school delinquency and non-alcoholics with no history of school delinquency significant at p<.01 level.
[b] Difference between alcoholics with history of school delinquency and non-alcoholics with no history of school delinquency significant at p<.05 level.
(From Dis. Nerv. Syst. 29: 238-243, 1968. Reprinted by permission.)

quency or alcoholism had intermediate rates of felony convictions. Similarly, alcoholism was twice as frequent among male relatives who had been convicted of felonies as among those without such convictions, and the alcoholism among the former relatives was more severe (Table 41).

143

TABLE 41
FELONY CONVICTIONS VS ALCOHOLISM (52)
(MALES ONLY)

	Interviewed Relatives		Noninterviewed Relatives	
	Felons (N=11)	Others (N=91)	Felons (N=29)	Others (N=129)
Alcoholics*	64% †	30%	38% ‡	13%
Mean Number of Alcoholic Symptoms	(N=7)	(N=27)		
Among the Alcoholics (Maximum = 17)	9.7 †	5.3		

* Includes definite and questionable alcoholics.
† Difference between the two values significant at p<.05 level.
‡ Difference between the two values significant at p<.01 level.

(From Dis. Nerv. Syst. *29:* 238-243, 1968. Reprinted by permission.)

The findings in Chapters 4 and 5 concerning the frequency of alcoholism and drug dependence and their roles in recidivism indicated certain noteworthy differences as well as similarities. The frequency of alcoholism was similar in male and female felons, but alcoholism was associated with increased criminal recidivism only for male felons. Drug dependence, on the other hand, while associated with increased criminal recidivism in both male and female felons, was much more frequent among female felons. Because the study of female felons was carried out about ten years later than the study of male felons, it is not possible to estimate how much of the sex difference in drug dependence was simply the result of the increasing prevalence of drug dependence in the community, rather than the result of sex-related factors, such as the likelihood that women criminals represent a more deviant segment of the female population than do male criminals of the male population (16, 17).

Further studies (currently underway) of new cohorts of male and female criminals are needed before sociocultural and sex differences can be correctly evaluated and compared. But while the relative importance of drug dependence may be increasing and may be playing a greater role in female criminality, the major impact of alcoholism in both sexes should not be ignored. The data indicate, in fact, that it is usually not alcoholism *or* drug dependence but alcoholism *and* drug dependence.

FINAL COMMENT

One of the unexpected results of these studies was the evidence of an association between sociopathy and hysteria. This finding, if confirmed, is of considerable theoretical importance. It would account for the striking sex differences in the two disorders. In addition, it would suggest that these differences are limited to overt manifestations, and that underlying etiologic and pathogenetic processes are similar. Additional lines of research are suggested by the finding. Parallel sociological, psychological, clinical, and biological investigations should be carried out for both conditions. The possibility that the same causal factors will result in different clinical pictures, depending on the sex of the individual, raises many interesting questions. What are the important biological and cultural factors contributing to the sex differences? To what extent will changes in the status of women affect this sex difference? Can the sex difference be used to identify the most important features of culture and family life related to the pathogenesis of the two conditions?

The basic methods of these investigations—systematic selection of subjects, description, diagnosis, follow-up, and family study—not only contribute to the consistency and validity of the results, but lead to observations that may facilitate an understanding of etiology and pathogenesis. No greater validation could be expected.

References

1. Arkonac, O., and Guze, S. B. A family study of hysteria. *N.E.J.M.* *268:* 239-242, 1963.
2. Arthurs, R., and Cahoon, E. A clinical and electroencephalographic survey of psychopathic personality. *Am. J. Psychiatry* *120:* 875-877, 1964.
3. Ashley, M. C. Outcome of one thousand cases paroled from the Middletown State Homeopathic Hospital. *State Hospital Quarterly* (New York) *8:* 64-70, 1922.
4. Banay, R. S. Alcoholism and crime. *Q. J. Stud. Alcohol 2:* 686-716, 1942.
5. Beckner, M. *The Biological Way of Thought.* New York: Columbia University Press, 1959.
6. Brill, H., and Malzberg, B. Statistical report based on the arrest record of 5,354 male ex-patients released from New York State Mental Hospitals during the period 1946-48. Mimeographed manuscript.
7. Bromberg, W., and Thompson, C. B. The relation of psychosis, mental defect and personality types to crime. *Journal of Criminal Law and Criminology 28:* 70-89, 1937.
8. Cantwell, D. P. Psychiatric illness in the families of hyperactive children. *Arch. Gen. Psychiatry 27:* 414-418, 1972.

147

References

9. Cassidy, W. L., Flanigan, M. B., Spellman, M., and Cohen, M. E. Clinical observations in manic depressive disease. A quantitative study of 100 manic-depressive patients and 50 medically sick controls. *J.A.M.A. 164:* 1535-1546, 1953.

10. Christiansen, K. O. Crime in a Danish twin population. *Acta Genet, Med. Gemellol. 19:* 323-326, 1970.

11. Cleckley, H. *Mask of Sanity.* St. Louis: C. V. Mosby, 1950.

12. Cloninger, C. R., and Guze, S. B. Psychiatric illness and female criminality: The role of sociopathy and hysteria in the antisocial woman. *Am. J. Psychiatry 127:* 303-311, 1970.

13. Cloninger, C. R., and Guze, S. B. Female criminals: Their personal, familial, and social backgrounds. *Arch. Gen. Psychiatry 23:* 554-558, 1970.

14. Cloninger, C. R., and Guze, S. B. Psychiatric disorders and criminal recidivism: A follow-up study of female criminals. *Arch. Gen. Psychiatry 29:* 266-269, 1973.

15. Cloninger, C. R., and Guze, S. B. Psychiatric illness in the families of female criminals: A study of 288 first-degree relatives. *Br. J. Psychiatry 122:* 697-703, 1973.

16. Cloninger, C. R., Reich, T., and Guze, S. B. The multifactorial model of disease transmission: 2. Sex differences in the familial transmission of sociopathy (antisocial personality). *Br. J. Psychiatry.* To be published in July 1975.

17. Cloninger, C. R., Reich, T., and Guze, S. B. The multifactorial model of disease transmission: 3. Familial relationship between sociopathy and hysteria (Briquet's Syndrome). *Br. J. Psychiatry.* To be published in July 1975.

18. Cohen, L. H., and Freeman, H. How dangerous to the community are state hospital patients? *Conn. State Medical Journal 9:* 697-700, 1945.

19. Cramer, M. J., and Blacker, E. J. "Early" and "late" problem drinkers among female prisoners. *J. of Health and Human Behavior 4:* 282-290, 1963.

20. Crowe, R. R. An adoption study of antisocial personality. *Arch. Gen. Psychiatry 31:* 785-791, 1974.

21. Cushman, P., Jr. Relationship between narcotic addiction and crime. *Federal Probation 38:* 38-43, 1974.

22. Edwards, G., Hensman, C., and Pedo, J. Drinking problems among recidivist prisoners. *Psychol. Med. 1:* 388-399, 1971.

23. Feighner, J. P., Robins, E., Guze, S. B., Woodruff, R. A., Wino-

kur, G., and Munoz, R. Diagnostic criteria for use in psychiatric research. *Arch. Gen. Psychiatry 26:* 57-63, 1972.

24. Feinstein, A. R. *Clinical Judgment.* Baltimore: Williams and Wilkins, 1967.

25. Feinstein, A. R., Pritchett, J., Schimpff, C. R., and Spitz, H. The epidemiology of cancer therapy. I. Clinical problems of statistical surveys. *Arch. Intern. Med. 123:* 171-186, 1969.

26. Feinstein, A. R., Pritchett, J., Schimpff, C. R., and Spitz, H. The epidemiology of cancer therapy. II. The clinical course: data, decision, and temporal demarcation. *Arch. Intern. Med. 123:* 323-344, 1969.

27. Feinstein, A. R., Pritchett, J., Schimpff, C. R., and Spitz, H. The epidemiology of cancer therapy. III. The management of imperfect data. *Arch. Intern. Med. 123:* 448-461, 1969.

28. Feinstein, A. R., Pritchett, J., Schimpff, C. R., and Spitz, H. The epidemiology of cancer therapy. IV. The extraction of data from medical records. *Arch. Intern. Med. 123:* 571-590, 1969.

29. Forrest, A. D. The differentiation of hysterical personality from hysterical psychopathy. *Br. J. Med. Psychol. 40:* 65-78, 1967.

30. Ganser, D. The Ganser Syndrome. *Br. J. Criminology 5:* 120-131, 1965.

31. Geis, G. *White-Collar Criminal.* New York: Atherton Press, 1968.

32. Gibbens, T. C. N., and Silberman, M. Alcoholism among prisoners. *Psychol. Med. 1:* 73-78, 1970.

33. Gillies, H. Murder in the West of Scotland. *Br. J. Psychiatry 111:* 1087-1094, 1965.

34. Glueck, B. A study of 608 admissions to Sing Sing Prison. *Mental Hygiene 2:* 85-151, 1918.

35. Glueck, S., and Glueck, E. *Predicting Delinquency and Crime.* Cambridge, Mass.: Harvard University Press, 1959.

36. Goldstein, A. S. *The Insanity Defense.* New Haven: Yale University Press, 1967.

37. Goodwin, D. W., Crane, J. B., and Guze, S: B. Felons who drink: An 8-year follow-up. *Q. J. Stud. Alcohol 32:* 136-147, 1971.

38. Guze, S. B. Conversion symptoms in criminals. *Am. J. Psychiatry 121:* 580-583, 1964.

39. Guze, S. B. A study of recidivism based upon a follow-up of 217 consecutive criminals. *J. Nerv. Ment. Dis. 138:* 575-580, 1964.

40. Guze, S. B. The diagnosis of hysteria: What are we trying to do? *Am. J. Psychiatry 124:* 491-498, 1967.

41. Guze, S. B. The role of follow-up studies: Their contribution to diagnostic classification as applied to hysteria. *Semin. Psychiatry* 2: 392-402, 1970.

42. Guze, S. B. The need for toughmindedness in psychiatric thinking. *South. Med. J. 63:* 662-671, 1970.

43. Guze, S. B., and Cantwell, D. P. Alcoholism, parole observations and criminal recidivism: A study of 116 parolees. *Am. J. Psychiatry 122:* 436-439, 1965.

44. Guze, S. B., and Goodwin, D. W. Diagnostic consistency in antisocial personality. *Am. J. Psychiatry 128:* 360-361, 1971.

45. Guze, S. B., and Goodwin, D. W. The consistency of the drinking history and the diagnosis of alcoholism. *Q. J. Stud. Alcohol 33:* 111-116, 1972.

46. Guze, S. B., Goodwin, D. W., and Crane, J. B. Criminality and psychiatric disorders. *Arch. Gen. Psychiatry 20:* 583-591, 1969.

47. Guze, S. B., Goodwin, D. W., and Crane, J. B. Criminal recidivism and psychiatric illness. *Am. J. Psychiatry 127:* 832-835, 1970.

48. Guze, S. B., Goodwin, D. W., and Crane, J. B. A psychiatric study of the wives of convicted felons: An example of assortative mating. *Am. J. Psychiatry 126:* 1773-1776, 1970.

49. Guze, S. B., Tuason, V. B., Gatfield, P. D., Stewart, M. A., and Picken, B. Psychiatric illness and crime with particular reference to alcoholism: A study of 223 criminals. *J. Nerv. Ment. Dis. 134:* 512-521, 1962.

50. Guze, S. B., Tuason, V. B., Stewart, M. A., and Picken, B. The drinking history: A comparison of reports by subjects and their relatives. *Q. J. Stud. Alcohol 24:* 249-260, 1963.

51. Guze, S. B., Wolfgram, E. D., McKinney, J. K., and Cantwell, D. P. Psychiatric illness in the families of convicted criminals: A study of 519 first-degree relatives. *Dis. Nerv. Syst. 28:* 651-659, 1967.

52. Guze, S. B., Wolfgram, E. D., McKinney, J. K., and Cantwell, D. P. Delinquency, social maladjustment, and crime: The role of alcoholism. (A study of first-degree relatives of convicted criminals). *Dis. Nerv. Syst. 29:* 238-243, 1968.

53. Guze, S. B., Woodruff, R. A., and Clayton, P. J. Secondary affective disorders: A study of 95 cases. *Psychol. Med. 1:* 426-428, 1971.

54. Guze, S. B., Woodruff, R. A., Jr., and Clayton, P. J. A study of

conversion symptoms in psychiatric outpatients. *Am. J. Psychiatry 128:* 643-646, 1971.
55. Guze, S. B., Woodruff, R. A., Jr., and Clayton, P. J. Hysteria and antisocial behavior: Further evidence of an association. *Am. J. Psychiatry 127:* 957-960, 1971.
56. Guze, S. B., Woodruff, R. A., Jr., and Clayton, P. J. Psychiatric disorders and criminality. *J.A.M.A. 227:* 641-642, 1974.
57. Häfner, H., and Böker, W. Mentally disordered violent offenders. *Soc. Psychiatry 8:* 220-229, 1973.
58. Hippocrates. *The Theory and Practice of Medicine.* New York: Philosophical Library, 1964.
59. Hook, E. B. Behavioral implications of the human XYY genotype. *Science 179:* 139-150, 1973.
60. Jellinek, E. M. Phases of alcohol addiction. *Q. J. Stud. Alcohol 13:* 673-684, 1952.
61. Kelley, C. R. *Crime in the United States.* Uniform Crime Reports (FBI), Washington, D.C.: U.S. Government Printing Office, 1972.
62. Kinsey, A. C., Pomeroy, W. B., and Martin, C. E. *Sexual Behavior in the Human Male.* Philadelphia: W. B. Saunders, 1948.
63. Kinsey, A. C., Pomeroy, W. B., Martin, C. E., and Gebhard, P. H. *Sexual Behavior in the Human Female.* Philadelphia: W. B. Saunders, 1953.
64. Langfeldt, G. The prognosis of schizophrenia. *Acta Psychiatr. et Neurol. Scand.* (Suppl.) 110, 1956.
65. Layzer, D. Heritability analyses of IQ scores: Science or numerology? *Science 183:* 1259-1266, 1974.
66. Maddocks, P. D. A five year follow-up of untreated psychopaths. *Br. J. Psychiatry 116:* 511-515, 1970.
67. Matthews, A. R., Jr. *Mental Disability and the Criminal Law.* Chicago: American Bar Foundation, 1970.
68. Maule, H. G., and Cooper, J. Alcoholism and crime—a study of the drinking and criminal habits of 50 discharged prisoners. *Brit. J. Addict. 61:* 201-212, 1966.
69. Mendelson, W., Johnson, N., and Stewart, M. A. Hyperactive children as teenagers: A follow-up study. *J. Nerv. Ment. Dis. 153:* 273-279, 1971.
70. Morris, N. The future of imprisonment: Toward a punitive philosophy. *Michigan Law Rev. 72:* 1161-1180, 1974.

References

71. Morrison, J. R., and Stewart, M. A. A family study of the hyperactive child syndrome. *Biol. Psychiatry 3:* 189-195, 1971.
72. Morrison, J. R., and Stewart, M. A. The psychiatric status of the legal families of adopted hyperactive children. *Arch. Gen. Psychiatry 28:* 888-891, 1973.
73. Nicol, A. R., Gunn, J. C., Gristwood, J., Foggitt, R. H., and Watson, J. P. The relationship of alcoholism to violent behavior resulting in long-term imprisonment. *Br. J. Psychiatry 123:* 47-51, 1973.
74. Oltman, J. E., and Friedman, S. A psychiatric study of one hundred criminals. *J. Nerv. Ment. Dis. 93:* 16-41, 1941.
75. *Oxford English Dictionary*, Compact Edition. Oxford: Clarendon Press, 1971.
76. Perley, M., and Guze, S. B. Hysteria—The stability and usefulness of clinical criteria. *N.E.J.M. 266:* 421-426, 1962.
77. Piotrowski, K. W., Losacco, D., and Guze, S. B. Psychiatric disorders and crime: A study of pretrial psychiatric examinations. Submitted for publication.
78. Pollitt, J. Natural history of obsessional states: A study of 150 cases. *Br. Med. J. 1:* 194-198, 1957.
79. Pollock, H. M. Is the paroled patient a menace to the community? *Psychiatr. Q. 12:* 236-244, 1938.
80. President's Commission on Law Enforcement and Administration of Justice. *The Challenge of Crime in a Free Society*. Washington, D.C.: U.S. Govt. Printing Office, 1967.
81. Purtell, J. J., Robins, E., and Cohen, M. E. Observations on clinical aspects of hysteria. *J.A.M.A. 146:* 902-909, 1951.
82. Rappeport, J., and Lassen, G. Dangerousness—Arrest rate comparisons of discharged patients and the general population. *Am. J. Psychiatry 121:* 776-783, 1965.
83. Rappeport, J., and Lassen, G. The dangerousness of female patients: A comparison of the arrest rate of discharged psychiatric patients and the general population. *Am. J. Psychiatry 123:* 413-419, 1966.
84. Reiss, A. J. *Occupations and Social Status*. Glencoe, Illinois: Free Press, 1961.
85. Robins, E., and Guze, S. B. Classification of affective disorders: The primary-secondary, the endogenous-reactive, and the neurotic-psychotic concepts. In *Recent Advances in Psychobiology of the Depressive Illnesses*, Williams, T. A., Katz, M. M., and

Shield, J. A., Jr., Editors. Washington, D.C.: U.S. Government Printing Office No. 70-9053, 1972.

86. Robins, L. *Deviant Children Grown Up.* Baltimore: Williams and Wilkins, 1966.

87. Satterfield, J. H., Cantwell, D. P., and Satterfield, B. T. Pathophysiology of the hyperactive child syndrome. *Arch. Gen. Psychiatry 31:* 839-844, 1974.

88. Schulsinger, F. Psychopathy, heredity, and environment. *Int. J. Ment. Health 1:* 190-206, 1972.

89. Selling, L. S. The psychiatric findings in the cases of 500 traffic offenders and accident-prone drivers. *Am. J. Psychiatry 97:* 68-79, 1940.

90. Silverman, D. Psychotic criminal: Study of 500 cases. *J. Clin. Psychopath. 8:* 301-327, 1946.

91. Slater, E., and Cowie, V. *The Genetics of Mental Disorders.* London: Oxford University Press, 1971.

92. Sokal, R. R. Classification: Purposes, principles, progress, prospects. *Science 185:* 1115-1123, 1974.

93. Steinbeck, J. *East of Eden.* New York: Viking Press, 1952.

94. Stephens, J. H., and Astrup, C. Prognosis in "process" and "nonprocess" schizophrenia. *Am. J. Psychiatry 119:* 945-953, 1963.

95. Thompson, C. B. A psychiatric study of recidivists. *Am. J. Psychiatry 94:* 591-604, 1937.

96. Tinklenberg, J. Drugs and crime. A consultant's report prepared for the National Commission on Marihuana and Drug Abuse, Oct. 1972.

97. Tupin, J. P., Mahar, D., and Smith, D. Two types of violent offenders with psychosocial descriptors. *Dis. Nerv. Syst. 34:* 356-363, 1973.

98. West, D. J. *Murder Followed by Suicide.* London: Heinemann, 1965.

99. Wheeler, E. O., White, P. D., Reed, E. W., and Cohen, M. E. Neurocirculatory asthenia (anxiety neurosis, effort syndrome, neurasthenia). *J.A.M.A. 142:* 878-889, 1950.

100. Wiersma, D. Crime and schizophrenics. *Exerpta Criminologica 6:* 168-181, 1966.

101. Woerner, P. I., and Guze, S. B. A family and marital study of hysteria. *Br. J. Psychiatry 114:* 161-168, 1968.

102. Wolfgang, M. E. *Patterns in Criminal Homicide.* Philadelphia: University of Pennsylvania Press, 1958.

References

103. Woodruff, R. A., Jr., Goodwin, D. W., and Guze, S. B. *Psychiatric Diagnosis*. New York: Oxford University Press, 1974.
104. Zimring, F. E. Measuring the impact of pretrial diversion from the criminal justice system. *U. of Chicago Law Rev.* *41:* 224-241, 1974.

Appendix A

Code No. _____ Hospital Chart No. _____

                               Hospital Registration No. _____

                               Clinic No. _____

Name: _____

Maiden Name(s): _____

Address: _____

Telephone: _____

Examiner: _____ Date: _____ Length of Exam: _____

                        Identifying Data

Age _____   Usual occupation _____

Birthdate _____   Current occupation _____

Sex _____   Spouse's occupation _____

Race _____   Spouse's schooling _____

           Parents: _____   Father's occupation _____
Religion Patient: _____

Marital state _____

Birthplace _____

Husband's or wife's name _____

Patient's business name, phone, and address _____

_____

Spouse's business name, phone, and address _____

_____

Referring physician's name, phone, and address _____

_____

Presenting Complaints

(Make a list of these; indicate with a "cc" the chief complaint(s), and indicate with an "MD" the iatrotropic complaint(s).)

Present Illness

Past Medical and Psychiatric History

Hospitalizations, Operations, Injuries
Operations (including tonsillectomy)
(Be sure to specifically inquire about childhood hospitalizations)

Date   Time in hospital   Why   Where   Operation

Nonsurgical Hospitals (Not including normal OB)
Date   Time in hospital   Where   Why

Mental Hospitals
(sanitarium, state hospital, mental hospital, rest home, and psychiatric units of general hospitals like Renard)

Date   Time in hospital   Hospital Name   Why

_____Number of nonsurgical general hospitalizations

_____Number of surgical hospitalizations

_____Total number of general hospitalizations (medical and surgical)

_____Number mental hospitalizations

_____Total number of hospitalizations

_____Number injuries (doctor, missed work, coma, bad scars)

Symptom Inventory

General criteria for scoring a symptom as positive.

A. The symptom led the patient to go to a physician.

B. The symptom was disabling. Disability is defined as the patient's
    report that the symptom caused him to make changes in his life
    because of the symptom. These changes include job troubles,
    trouble sleeping, need for rest, need for help when such was not
    ordinarily needed, restrictions of social and recreational life,
    and a belief by the patient that the symptom definitely made a
    difference in his life even though he cannot pinpoint the differ-
    ence.

C. The symptom led the patient to take medication.

D. The physician believes because of its clinical importance the
    symptom should be scored as positive even though it does not
    fulfil criteria A, B, or C. For example, a spell of blindness
    lasting a few minutes which the patient may minimize, i.e., deny
    that criteria A through C apply, would be scored as positive.
    This criterion is also meant to include any symptom that the
    physician believes to be of clinical significance to him, with-
    out regard to its fulfilling criteria A, B, or C.

General instructions for recording responses to each symptom:

1. Any positive response must be elaborated with regard to its
    qualitative description, its frequency, and its chronology.

2. Any item to which the patient gives a tentative positive re-
    sponse but which is scored as negative must be elaborated so
    that the entire group can reach its own decision concerning the
    validity of the negative scoring.

_____ 1. Always sickly--majority of life (Patient's evaluation of self rather than the fact of being chronically ill.)

_____ 2. Nervousness

_____ 3. Dyspnea (Negative: [a] If on moderate to strenuous physical exertion. [b] If on mild exertion and not a recent change. Positive: [a] If not on exertion, regardless of the presence or absence of associated symptoms and of psychologic concomitants. [b] If on mild exertion and a recent change.)

_____ 4. Palpitation (Negative: [a] If on exertion and not a recent change. [b] If on severe and acute emotional stress only. Positive: [a] If on mild exertion and a recent change. [b] If not on exertion, regardless of the presence or absence of associated symptoms and psychologic concomitants.)

_____ 5. Chest pain (Chest as defined as the anterior, lateral, or posterior chest, excepting midline (vertebral) thoracic pain. The latter will be scored under back pain.)

_____ 6. Dizziness (Include dizziness on change of position if it meets the general criteria. Differentiate dizziness from vertigo.)

_____ 7. Vertigo

_____ 8. Headache (Include occipital and posterior cervical pain which goes to the occipital region.) (Negative: if any medication consists of simple analgesics like aspirin, anacin, bufferin, etc. and other criteria are absent.)

_____ 9. Anxiety attack (Positive: Spells of apprehension, fear, uneasiness, etc., plus symptoms from the following list, one of which must be dyspnea or palpitation: dyspnea, palpitation, weakness, sweating, dizziness, paresthesias, visual blurring, trembling. Negative: If the above symptoms have occurred only with unusual and acute emotion-provoking situations.)

_____10. Fatigue

_____11. Blindness (Any episode of complete absence of light perception lasting more than a fleeting instant. See general criterion D.)

_____12. Paralysis (Any episode of inability to move not due to pain, not numbness whether or not associated with numbness, lasting more than a minute or lasting seconds if it has occurred more than once. Cannot be explained by pressure on a peripheral nerve.)

_____13. Ataxia or trouble walking

_____14. Anesthesia (Cannot feel anything, whether or not associated with numbness and tingling, lasting more than a fleeting instant, and not explained by pressure on a peripheral nerve.)

_____15. Loss of voice (Negative: If associated with colds or infection or shouting only, no matter how frequently. Positive: Voice must be lost for 30 minutes or more. Voice loss is defined as muteness or whispering but not hoarseness.

_____16. Lump in throat (Negative: If when feels like crying only.)

_____17. Fits or convulsions or falling-out spells or dreamy spells (Convulsions--Grand mal, petit mal, Jacksonian seizures. Spells--Psychomotor seizures and spells for which patient is amnesic and in which he exhibits purposeless and random behavior.)

_____18. Other spells

_____19. Fainting spells (Positive: Only if premonitory symptoms such as warm, sweaty, weak, dizzy exist and if the patient regains consciousness within 1 minute. Must occur more than once.)

_____20. Unconsciousness (Negative: If related to fits, faints, amnesia, head injury. Positive: Any duration is sufficient.)

_____21. Amnesia (Positive: Apparently purposive and integrated movements occurring in a spell without a memory for the period. Negative: If related to alcohol score under alcoholic blackouts.)

_____22. Visual blurring (Negative: Excluding spots before the eyes. Also negative if related to refractive error.)

_____23. Diplopia

_____24. Deafness

_____25. Weakness

_____26. Weight loss (Positive: Weight loss of 10 pounds or more within a one year period when the patient was not dieting; if a recent loss of 2 pounds or more per week even if total loss is less than 10 pounds.)

_____27. Sudden gains or losses in weight (Positive: A belief by the patient that he has suddenly [less than 2 weeks] gained or lost more than 15 pounds in weight, not related to medical disease.)

_____28. Anorexia (Defined as appetite, not amount eaten.)

_____29. Nausea without vomiting

_____30. Vomiting

_____31. Abdominal pains (Exclude dysmenorrhea.)

_____32. Abdominal bloating and gas

_____33. Food intolerance (Positive: More than 1 symptom to at least 3 kinds of food.)

_____34. Diarrhea

_____35. Constipation

_____36. Painful urination

_____37. Urinary retention (Positive: If catheterized because of inability to void unrelated to surgery or childbirth or if after surgery or childbirth, must be catheterized for a week or longer.)

_____38. Menstrual pain (Patient says it was premarital only.) (for women who have been married)

_____39. Menstrual pain (Patient says it was pre-pregnancy only.)

_____40. Menstrual pain (Other)

Only one of these should be scored +

_____41. Menstrual irregularity including amenorrhea for at least 2 periods (Excluding first year after menarche and period just before menopause.)

_____42. Menstrual hemorrhage (Excluding 2 years prior to cessation of menstrual periods.)

_____43. Menopausal manifestations: if positive, give age at last menstruation.

_____44. Sexual indifference

_____45. Frigidity (Never have orgasm or less than once a year with regular intercourse.)

_____46. Frigidity (Orgasm only in a minority of episodes of coitus.)

_____47. Dyspareunia (Negative: If a medical reason exists.)

_____48. Diminished sex drive (Negative: If a very gradual loss with increasing age over age of 55, or if due to a disabling medical disease. Positive: 50% or greater reduction in frequency of intercourse not due to woman's refusal, etc., and lasting at least one month.)

_____49. Impotence (Positive: If in the majority of attempts over a minimum period of 2 months impotence occurs.)

_____50. Age at first sexual intercourse

_____51. Number of partners

_____52. Unfaithfulness (Number of partners--extramarital.)

_____53. Prostitution (Ask this only if sociopathy is suspected.)

_____54. Homosexuality (Experimented with sexual relations with same sex.)

_____55. Pregnancy vomiting (Positive: Vomiting all 9 months only or if hospitalized for vomiting.)

_____56. Irritable

_____57. Fighting before age 18 (In trouble two or more times.)

_____58. Fighting at or later than age 18 (more than once or once with a weapon.)

_____59. Did you ever run away from home overnight? (Dates.)

_____60. Ever have a wanderlust and travel from place to place? (Where?)

_____61. Insomnia

_____62. Hypersomnia

_____63. Back pain (Includes pain along vertebral column, in the sacroiliac regions, and in the costovertebral angles.)

_____64. Joint pain

_____65. Extremity pain

_____66. Burning pain (rectum, private parts, mouth)

_____67. Pains anywhere else in body

_____68. Depressed, sad, despondent, discouraged, blue, "down in the dumps"

_____69. Had to quit working (school) because felt so bad (sick, unhappy, etc.)

_____70. Trouble doing anything because you felt bad or it seemed so much trouble.

_____71. Cried a lot (Positive: Began to cry when previously did not or episodes of increased frequency of crying.)

_____72. Felt life was hopeless

Attempt to score 73, 74, and 75 in a mutually exclusive fashion, unless of course 2 or 3 thinking disturbances occur together.

_____73. Trouble thinking (Specifically inquire about rate: too fast or too slow or any other trouble not covered in 74 or 75.)

_____74. Trouble concentrating

_____75. Trouble with memory

_____76. Loss of interest and/or diminished activity (Newspapers, TV, movies, friends, family, job, church.)

_____77. Diurnal variation (Describe.)

_____78. Have you ever felt you were worthless or no good or sinful?

_____79. Morbid thoughts: thoughts of death or dying

_____80. Wanted to die

_____81. Thought of suicide (Defined as thinking about his own suicide.)

_____82. Tried suicide

_____83. Didn't feel like dressing up or keeping yourself as well-groomed (clean) as usual.

_____84. Have you ever had a time when you were too happy, too excited, too enthusiastic, overconfident, overactive, overtalkative?

_____85. Have you ever had a time when you went on spending sprees, or invested wildly?

_____86. Have you ever felt you were a person with a special mission in life?

_____87. Have you ever felt that you understood things other people can't?

_____88. Ever a time when you felt particularly strong and powerful?

_____89. Phobias (Heights, streets, dark, public conveyances, leaving home, closed places, disease, lues, heart disease, cancer, being alone, crowds, losing mind, dying, etc.)

_____90. Obsessions (Injure someone else, harm yourself, germs, disease, counting, indecision, doubting, etc.)

_____91. Compulsions (Handwashing, counting, not stepping on cracks, locks, gas, dressing, bathing, etc.)

_____92. Do you ever think people talk about you?

_____93. Do you ever think people watch you?

_____94. Do you ever think people follow you?

_____95. Anyone plotting against you? Trying to hurt you? Poison you?

_____96. Have you ever thought anyone was reading your mind?

_____97. Have you ever thought others can control your thinking?

_____98. Have you ever felt your thoughts were taken away?

_____99. Ever influenced in unusual ways? (T.V., radio, hypnosis, machine.)

_____100. Visual hallucinations?

_____101. Auditory hallucinations?

_____102. Olfactory hallucinations?

_____103. Peculiar sensations in body, genitals, skin?

_____104. Ever felt like another person? Changed into another person? Unreal? Dead? (Depersonalization.)

_____105. Have things about you seemed changed? Unreal? Different place? Hell? (Derealization.)

_____106. Any delusions including one of above or any others? If others, specify delusion.

FAMILY HISTORY REVIEW

Code as follows: A = Alive (A)= Alive and probably available
                  † = Deceased   ? Age

Relation Name	Address	Phone	Code	Psychiatric Info. ? Age
M.GrandF	XXXXXXXX	XXX		
M.GrandM	XXXXXXXX	XXX		
P.GrandF	XXXXXXXX	XXX		
P.GrandM	XXXXXXXX	XXX		
M.Aunts				
M.Uncles				
P.Aunts				
P.Uncles				
Father				
Mother				
Brothers:				
Sisters:				
Children:				

Note: If grandchildren older than 14 years old - record similar
information on p.

Family History

(Get a description so a diagnosis can be made. Include parents,
 siblings, children, grandparents, aunts and uncles, and grandchildren.)

_____ 1. Nervous (Neurosis)

_____ 2. Nervous Breakdown

_____ 3. Suicide

_____ 4. Attempted Suicide

_____ 5. Alcoholism

_____ 6. Drug Dependency (Addiction or abuse)

_____ 7. Consult a psychiatrist

_____ 8. Clinic or physician for Alcoholism

_____ 9. General Hospital for Alcoholism

_____ 10. Mental Hospital or Psychiatric Unit of General Hospital

_____ 11. Prison or Jail

_____ 12. Other antisocial or delinquent history

_____ 13. Other

SUMMARY:

_____ Number of siblings (including deceased)

_____ Patient's sibling rank (i.e., 3/5)

_____ Are you a twin? Score as follows:

             0 = negative
             1 = identical twin
             2 = fraternal twin
             3 = triplets

_____ Are there any twins or triplets in your
          family? (Record details)

Parental Home

	Age (now or at death)	Date of death & cause	Present Health	Psychiatric Illness
Father (and/or surrogates)				
Mother (and/or surrogates)				

Were parents or surrogates ever: (note patient's age)

_____1. Divorced?

_____2. Separated (three months or longer)?

Do not score "separated" as positive if parents were divorced.

Was either parent or surrogate: (patient's age, plus F for father, M for mother) (Get chronology. If step-parent or parent-surrogate in picture, same information for them. Indicate which one referred to: F, M, StepF, StepM, etc.)

_____3. A heavy drinker (or alcoholic)?

_____4. Jailed (especially for alcoholism)?

_____5. Not a steady worker?

Was subject ever:

_____6. In foster home? (dates)

_____7. In institution such as orphan's home? (dates)

_____8. Raised by relatives or friends? (dates)

Marital History

Current marital status:

_____	1. Married (not common law)	_____	5. Married common law
_____	2. Divorced	_____	6. Desertion
_____	3. Separated	_____	7. Widow
_____	4. Legal separation	_____	8. Never married

     9. List of marriages

Marriage No.	Inclusive Dates	How Ended	Reason for incompatibility (Ask whether have considered separation or divorce even if incompatibility is denied)

     10. Children

Rank	Sex	Marriage No.	Birth-date	Death Date	Present Address

_____ 11. Total number of children (including illegitimate: list above as well)

_____ 12. Number now living (including illegitimate)

Job History

1. What is your usual occupation? (Get description) _____

2. What is your present income from your work? (<u>Note whether take-home or gross</u>)

	Week	Month	Year
____a.	<$40	<$150	<$2000
____b.	$40-60	$150-250	$2000-3000
____c.	$60-100	$250-400	$3000-5000
____d.	$100-150	$400-600	$5000-7500
____e.	>$150	$600-800	$7500-10000
____f.			$10000-15000
____g.			>$15000
____h.	←————Unemployed————→		

3. Have you ever earned more? (For at least one year) _____
   How much? _____

4. What is the family income from all sources (wages, salaries, investments, etc.)--use range above _____

5. How long have you worked for your present employer? _____
   (Record details of job changes with same employer)

6. How many jobs have you had in the last ten years? (list jobs)
   _____

7. How many jobs in previous ten years? _____

8. What is the longest time you worked for anyone? _____

9. Age at which you started working (full-time) _____

10. Total number jobs (full-time) _____

11. Fired? (number of times, reasons) _____

12. Ever quit a job without having another to go to? _____

13. Any income from pensions? (ADC, Social Security, Welfare, OAA)
    (How long and how much?) _____

14. Any income from compensation--insurance, VA, job, due to injury or illness? (How long and how much?) _____

Military Service

_____ 1. Dates in service

_____ 2. Highest rank

_____ 3. Demotions

_____ 4. AWOL

_____ 5. Fines

_____ 6. Hospitalization

_____ 7. Court martial: Charge: Sentence:

_____ 8. Kind of discharge: (honorable, general, medical, without
                                honor, undesirable, dishonorable)

_____ 9. Reason for discharge

_____10. No military service. Reason?

School History

_____ 1. Grade completed

_____ 2. Age left school

_____ 3. Expelled or suspended

_____ 4. Truancy (average more than once a year except for last
             year in school in a school dropout, or if in trouble
             including truant officer)

_____ 5. Fights (leading to trouble with teachers, principal or
             other adults)

_____ 6. Failed a subject

_____ 7. Ever have to repeat a semester or a year

_____ 8. Out because of illness for most of a semester or a year

_____ 9. Ever have to see the principal

_____10. Ever have to have parents come to school for academic or
             disciplinary reason

_____11. Years of technical training programs attended

_____12. Names and locations of schools

Alcohol

(Get ages for each positive symptom)

_____ 1. Have you ever used alcohol?

_____ 2. How frequently? (Times/month)

_____ 3. Amount in ounces per week expressed as whiskey (1 oz. whiskey--3 oz. wine--8 oz. beer)

_____ 4. Has your family ever objected to your drinking?

_____ 5. Did you ever think you drank too much in general?

_____ 6. Have others ever said you drink too much for your own good? (Such as friends, physicians, clergymen, etc.)

_____ 7. Have you ever felt guilty about drinking?

_____ 8. Have you ever lost friends because of drinking?

_____ 9. Did you ever get into trouble at work because of drinking?

_____ 10. Did you ever lose a job on account of drinking?

_____ 11. Did you ever have trouble with auto driving (speeding, accident, etc.) because of drinking?

_____ 12. Have you ever been arrested, even for a few hours, because of drinking and/or disturbing the peace?

_____ 13. Have you ever gotten into fights when drinking?

_____ 14. Have you ever gone on benders? (48 hours of drinking associated with default of usual obligations: must have occurred more than once. There must be repetitive drinking bouts of at least 48 hours if no obligations are defaulted, i.e., while on leave from military service)

_____ 15. Have you ever wanted to stop drinking and couldn't?

_____ 16. Have you ever tried to control your drinking by trying to drink only under certain circumstances (time of day, places, associates)?

_____ 17. Did you ever drink before breakfast?

_____ 18. Did you ever drink unusual things such as hair tonic, paint solvent, rubbing alcohol?

_____ 19. Have you ever had memory losses when drinking? (Blackouts)

_____20. Have you ever experienced impotence associated with drinking?

_____21. Have you ever had the shakes associated with drinking?

_____22. Have you ever seen or heard things that weren't there associated with drinking?

_____23. Have you ever had fits associated with drinking?

_____24. Have you ever had DT's associated with drinking?

_____25. Have you ever had liver disease associated with drinking?

_____26. Did you ever consider joining AA?

_____27. Age started heavy drinking.

_____28. Age stopped heavy drinking.

Drugs

_____ 1. Do you ever take drugs for sleeping?

_____ 2. Every night?

_____ 3. During the day?

_____ 4. Do you ever take tranquilizers or nerve medicine?

_____ 5. Have you ever used marihuana?

_____ 6. Have you ever used "bennies," "yellow jackets," "acid," or "joy popped," or "main-lined"?

_____ 7. Do you think you ever took too many drugs?

_____ 8. Have you ever experimented with drugs?

_____ 9. Did you ever want to stop taking drugs and couldn't?

_____10. Were you ever addicted or habituated?

Arrests

_____ 1. Have you ever had trouble with the police? (Include juvenile troubles)

_____ 2. Were you ever in reform school, industrial school, detention home?

_____ 3. Have you ever been in workhouse, city or county jail, state pen., intermediate reform school, federal pen.?

Arrests	Date	Sentence	Time served	Where

_____ 4a. Parking tickets

_____ 4b. Traffic violation

_____ 5. Drinking

_____ 6. Disturbing the peace

_____ 7. Fighting

_____ 8. Robbery

_____ 9. Burglary

_____ 10. Forgery

_____ 11. Auto theft

_____ 12. Manslaughter

_____ 13. Voyeurism--exhibitionism

_____ 14. Larceny

_____ 15. Child molestation

_____ 16. Homosexuality

_____ 17. Vagrancy

_____ 18. Impersonating

_____ 19. Fraud (con man)

_____ 20. Drugs (taking or peddling)

_____ 21. Gambling

_____ 22. Murder

_____ 23. Rape

_____ 24. Embezzlement

_____ 25. Other

_____ 26. Did you ever have trouble with authorities in jail such as restriction of privileges, solitary, etc.?

Mental Status

A. General Appearance and Behavior

B. Speech

C. Mood

D. Content of Thought (Describe anything not described under the history)

E. Orientation

　　　_____1.　Time

　　　_____2.　Place

　　　_____3.　Person

F. Memory

G. Intellectual Function

H. Insight and Judgment (Include estimate of reliability of information obtained)

Significant Physical and
Laboratory Findings

Outside History

(In a chronic brain syndrome or delirious patient where most of the
history is taken from an outside source, indicate the source here but
fill in the interview blanks rather than putting the history here.
If only some supplemental information is obtained from an outside
source this supplemental information may be recorded here.)

Progress Notes and Follow-up

Index

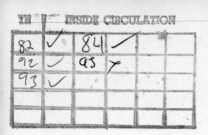

82	✓	84	✓		
92	✓	93	✓		
93	✓				